inner asia

inner asia

**A Collection of Travel Stories from
the Indian Subcontinent**

Kiva Bottero

THE MINDFUL WORD
www.themindfulword.org

Book design: Dew Media
"Spiritual Warriors" (p. 53): co-written with Are Saltveit

Most of the stories in this book are freely available on The Mindful Word. Visit www.themindfulword.org to read these and other articles and to sign up for our free monthly newsletter.

Note: Regarding the Bhutan section, the Tourism Council of Bhutan covered my expenses while I was in Bhutan. I was not told I had to write positive reviews and I was not told that I cannot write anything negative. The intention of the press trip was to familiarize the writer with the country so as to convey that information properly to readers. To properly write about a destination in travel writing means to have actually travelled there, which is not always the case in travel writing. This was a place I had wanted to write about, but given the financial reality of travel writing this was not a possibility without some form of financial assistance. This arrangement did not affect the objectivity of my writing in any way.

The Mindful Word
701-1120 Finch Ave. W. #928
Toronto, Ontario
M3J 3H7, Canada

ISBN 978-1-988245-74-4

Printed in the United States of America

Not until we are lost do we begin to understand ourselves.
HENRY DAVID THOREAU

CONTENTS

BHUTAN

SRI LANKA

NEPAL

INTRODUCTION

SHORTLY AFTER I LANDED in India I met a couple who had been to the country so many times they had lost count. About twenty times they told me. I ended up meeting many Indiaphiles like this.

It wasn't long before I too found out what the Indiaphiles were raving about. But I also found out what those who consider India to be an acronym for "I'll Never Do It Again" were thinking.

It's those two opposites that make the country so damn intriguing. By experiencing such extremes we get to know so much, so quickly. It's a place where time has a way of morphing to accommodate the mass of experience that one can cram in.

From beholding the towering heights of the Himalayas to hearing the captivating sounds of a classical Indian raga to savouring the delectable tastes of a dosa there's just so much to digest on this subcontinent.

These things are all wonderful, but they're all just things. To see, touch, hear, smell, taste. What is truly remarkable about this region exists beyond the senses. It's the invisible force that underlies what we observe on the surface.

It is sitting in a car driving among a crush of other cars, autorickshaws and motorbikes, eight vehicles abreast and who knows how many vehicles deep, driving directly into a phalanx of an equal amount of metal, rubber, skin and bones—then without the aid of lanes, traffic signals or the faintest hint of authority, the weaving just magically happens without accident.

Or sitting on the roof of a monastery in the middle of nowhere Himalayas and hearing the sound of nothing but the lone voice in your head that suddenly delivers an offering of contemplative wisdom in gratitude for giving it some much needed silence.

Few places in the world can transform a person the way India does. And if you're someone who's into the things India has spawned like Yoga or Buddhism, the power this place can deliver is truly beyond compare.

Inner Asia is a celebration of the transformative potential of the Indian subcontinent. It is also a contemplation on how this region is itself being rapidly transformed through the practicalities of modern living.

In the three years I was there I wrote a number of stories, some of which I've compiled into this book. Some of these stories are personal reflections on a place. What I learned from being there, what I understood the place to be, how I changed. Others were written purely from a fascination with a place and a desire to express that fascination, serving as useful travel recommendations. I've also written narratives about others who are living and working in the region that offer a peek into their interesting lives. To round it off, this compilation of stories includes think pieces that attempt to interpret the culture and way of life in general.

I can't think of anywhere on Earth that rivals the awe, the magic and the power of this magnificent place.

It's a place that captured my heart and soul and urged me to write and write and now I turn it over to you to read and read. To be inspired to explore and understand this fascinating part of the world.

india

A SYMPHONY OF CACOPHONY

Walking the streets of India

IN INDIA THE word "bad" doesn't hold much meaning. For a country of 1.2 billion there's not much room to move, which means a lot of traffic and a lot of faith. A spectacle that the many street dwellers get to absorb day after day. Today I am enveloped in this spectacle.-

One tiny speck walking among a horde of humanity, I amble along the main road adjacent to the Ganga River in Varanasi. As I approach a large chowk (square) near the bazaar, the traffic thickens.

Rickshaws and bicycles putter along at pedal pace, about the speed traffic usually moves. Helmetless motorcyclists—rarely one, usually two, three, four or more to a motorcycle—weave in and out among clunky cars. Unfit for these roads, these moving boxes of steel and glass are dimpled, scratched and worn with the weight of traffic that pushes up against it, but rarely seriously dented. Even more beat up are the autorickshaws, their eager drivers always with one eye on the road, one on the throng of potential customers walking alongside.

Human traffic is only half of the equation. Suicidal dogs zip in between the whole mess of vehicles and people, packs of monkeys occupy the airspace, scampering along loosely strung telephone wires—like bands of gypsies they always seem to be evading stones from cursing street merchants below.

Whether it's because they know they're considered sacred and protected by law, because of their calm demeanor, or a bit of both, the cows are the only ones completely unfazed, sitting like roadblocks in the middle of the street or lumbering along the sidelines rooting through trash.

3

I take three steps forward, sidestep around stopped cars. Forward again. Stop. Back up to avoid getting smacked by an auto. Lurch around a moped that just pulled in front and slowly arrive at the chowk.

Without traffic lights, the multi-rhythmic mass of humanity, cattle, doggerel, steel, glass and rubber fends for itself. Like molecules of water making their way through a drain clogged with hair and grime, the vehicles all come together from different directions, ebbing and flowing around each other, always within inches. It may be a slow affair, but with a lot of eye contact and some shouting and honking, eventually everyone gets through. A task that is easily completed in most countries, in India demands a merging of minds and the skill of an all-star Tetris player.

Half step by half step I follow single file behind a man and a woman. Our little pedestrian clump faces the turnabout. We get a quarter of the way through until we're forced in the middle of complete gridlock, layers of vehicles surrounding us. For twenty seconds the man in front directs traffic around him. It is up to him to break the gridlock. He does then passes through. The woman takes his spot as traffic cop and waves a couple of vehicles along before making her way. My turn through the crush. I give a motorcycle the green light, hold up my hand to another and scoot past, smiling at the small role the pedestrian plays in moving traffic along.

Organized chaos. A term that aptly describes India in a lot of ways. A paradox that Mother India alone can sort out. I look at a cow lying on the street as motorcycles whiz by within inches of it. If it had feathers not a single one would be ruffled. Who needs traffic lights when you have this majestic reminder of peace? Sacred Nandi directing traffic—not stop and go, turn left or turn right, but be peaceful and remain calm, accept the traffic or stay at home. It's a "system" that more or less works.

Not even a month later I was at that same intersection, except this time it was completely different. Like pumped up thoroughbreds at the starting line, row upon row of revved up traffic was waiting at a stoplight. Where once there was organized chaos, now there is a mechanical pilot telling people where to go, what to do. Telling the multitude how to live their lives as separate beings no longer needing to embrace the wonder of coherence. Is this progress getting the green light or religion getting slammed on the brakes? If cows could speak I think they'd say their time here is done.

LESSONS AT VARANASI

Reflecting on life and death in India's most sacred city

WRAPPED IN A WHITE SARI, she sat cross-legged on her paper thin mat waiting to die. The solemn look on her deeply creased face complemented her hunched over posture. It was the look of a lifetime of poverty in India. Her diminutive frame crumpled by the weight of a hard life occupied almost no space in the cavernous concrete structure, a hospice overlooking the sacred Ganga River.

Soon it would be her turn to die. And according to Hindu belief, she was in the best place for it: Varanasi. The holiest of India's cities. Having spawned Ravi Shankar, Kabir and other great artists, Varanasi is known for its vibrant arts scene. It is known for its fine silk and clothing. It is known for its temples. But above all else it is known for its cremation ritual, a non-stop sacred spectacle on the *ghats* (river embankments) of the Ganga.

Pulled by poignant images of this centuries-old ritual, I had arrived in Varanasi curious and ready for anything. Since my mother had died when I was a young adult I had felt somehow closer to death. Connected to it and always keen to learn lessons from it.

As I approached the main burning ghat a young man warned me not to take photos of the cremation, speaking with the authority of someone who worked there. In a city where you can't walk more than a minute before being asked if you want to hire a boat, get a massage, have your ears cleaned or buy some drugs, the touts have to be aggressive or else they won't get anywhere, so I thought he was trying to sell me something. But he introduced himself as a volunteer, saying he wanted no cash. It was a good service he does

7

too, since the ghats have inevitably become a tourist attraction that locals are surprisingly OK with considering they're grieving close family and friends.

He passed me off to the hospice manager who led me to a grim looking concrete shell of a building. No windows or finishings of any kind, just a bare cold structure. It didn't look like much and was equally uninviting from the inside. But it had a view.

From this high point, the woman in white and a cluster of other elders had front row seats to a steady stream of death and a time lapse photograph of decay. They sat on hard concrete floors, talking little—the silence forcing them to contemplate what soon would become their own fate, pleased knowing that they've upped the odds of ending the cycle of life and death by dying in the sacred heart centre of India. How long they sit is only up to the universe to decide.

And what a fitting way it is to spend your last days. Whether you've spent any amount of time contemplating death, you're inevitably contemplating life. You're asking the big questions: "Who am I? What am I here for? What is my purpose in life?

As I looked out the windowless opening in the building, I inhaled smoky air thick with the weight of grief. Death and decay were all around, but it did not smell of death and decay thanks to the bodies being carefully prepared with *ghee* (clarified butter).

The tools of the cremation trade were all right around the burning ghat. One armful after another, strong men carried heaps of wood to even stronger men who chopped the wood all day. *Brahmin* priests dressed all in white with shaved heads save for a little tail of hair at the top blessed the bodies with reverence while the *dom* (members of the untouchable caste) did the dirty work, routinely stoking the fire and flipping the bodies like burgers on a barbeque.

The hospice manager told me about the plight of the poor who die in Varanasi. They cannot afford to buy enough wood so their half-charred remains are dumped into the Ganga, adding to the mess of one of the most polluted rivers in the world. Varanasi had a wise idea awhile back: fill the river with flesh-eating turtles, but that pretty much flopped when the turtles got poached. They tried pushing a crematorium as an alternative, but that just didn't have the same allure as the traditional cremation ritual.

The woman in white put her hands on my head and blessed me, chanting a number of words in Hindi. With the manager translating, she asked me for the names of my family members so I could extend the blessing to them. Afterwards, he asked for a great sum of money to pay for wood for her. I offered some money, not nearly as much as he asked for, and left, heading below for a closer look.

Deceased *brahmins* (highest caste of priests and scholars) scored the preferred spots higher up from the river and the untouchable castes were forced down to the bank of the river, which was thick with the muck of cow dung, ashes and who knows what else.

Buddhist monk Thich Nhat Hanh's teachings on death and impermanence jolted to mind as I took in the scene. I repeated a shortened version of one of his *gathas* (mindfulness practice verses): breathing in I see my dead body, breathing out I smile at my dead body, as I visualized my deceased body being burned to ashes.

This visualization, like his other gathas, instilled a sense of peace in me. Intellectually I had known that everything is impermanent, but somehow standing among these bodies being burned out in the open right beside men washing their clothes and cows grazing through the rubbish, just felt so… natural. Not some far-off, melancholic event shrouded by closed caskets to be buried in the ground, but present. Real.

What amplified the feeling of impermanence was living as just one of this country's 1.2 billion, liberated from any need to individualize. The jaws of reality bit hard: just be as I am right here with whatever I've got and as whoever I am. Just be every day until I die. And when I die… poof. Gone just the way I came.

As I walked away from the ghat and winded my way through the ancient city's labyrinthine alleys, I still felt connected to the scene at the river. A regular stream of bodies being paraded on bamboo stretchers by family members chanted, "*Rama nama satya hai. Rama nama satya hai*" (the name of god is truth). A solemn reminder of death that charged the city's atmosphere with life.

9

The more we understand death, the more we appreciate life. Almost every time I talk to my 91-year-old grandmother she tells me to "enjoy your life" which reminds me of the aphorism, "Live every day as if it's your last." This reminder first came to me as a parting gift from my mother's premature death and has since been regifted to me time and again. And it is a reminder that's there for anyone who wants to reflect on the uncomfortable thought of death. An uncomfortable reminder that is played out in the open for all to see every minute of every day in Varanasi.

CLEARLY COMPASSIONATE

Seeing the Dalai Lama lights the way to true compassion

YOUNG POPLAR TREES scatter the sunlight into patches of shade in the courtyard of the Main Temple in Dharamsala, India—home of the Buddhist spiritual leader and the Tibetan government-in-exile.

A mixed crowd, equal parts monastic, tourist (Indian and Westerners) and Tibetan exiles sit in anticipation of the Dalai Lama's arrival. A young Tibetan father chases his infant son who's running from group to group touching everything in sight. Elders sit with their families and friends, prayer beads in hand, talking quietly or praying. Westerners sit alone or in small groups of two or three, mostly reading or sitting in silence.

The way lightning charges the atmosphere signalling an approaching storm, a buzz charges the air. The ocean of humanity swells together and moves to the gate, joining the dozens already waiting.

A Tibetan security guard with the international standard military-style buzz cut motions to get down. The front of the throng comply, sitting or bowing deeply, hands together in front of their faces, heads craned up, eyes fixed on the entrance. Unlike the frenzied excitement that accompanies a visit by an A-list member of the entertainment industry, this excitement's a tranquil one.

A plainclothes Indian police officer leads the entourage, a rifle strapped to his right shoulder, finger not far from the trigger. The busy eyes of the security guard dart from one spot to another.

His Holiness arrives. With this signature smile he passes the flame from his torch of everlasting joy to the many willing candles

11

bowed before him. One by one, he lights the candles with glowing smiles of delight. The Westerners in particular beam wide smiles. The courtyard's charged with His Holiness' light.

On this second of three days of teaching, he covers the basics of Buddhism at the request of the Indian sangha from his seat in the temple with more than 2,000 spread out within and outside the temple on two floors. Non-Tibetans tune in their $4 made-in-China hand-held radios as the translator crackles through the low-frequency signal. His Holiness speaks in Tibetan then gets translated into a few of the more commonly spoken languages. The mixed crowd of Tibetan and non-Tibetan speakers take turns tuning in and tuning out.

His teachings are clear and direct. He cuts through the complexities of Buddhist philosophy to speak to the commoner. Despite being elevated to godlike status by his Tibetan followers, he remains ever humble, putting himself on par with others.

In five- to ten-minute increments he pieces together the basics of shamatha meditation—right from the basics: hold right hand on top of the left, thumbs together, held at navel—to explaining the nature of impermanence.

"The body is always changing so people think 'I' is the mind. But a German brain scientist at the Brain-Mind conference pointed out that if there was an 'I' in the brain, it would have to be the brain's control centre, but there is no control centre, the brain works independently," he explains, as he often does, from another person's perspective to help people better relate to his teachings.

The session ends and the familiar buzz of excitement again charges the crowd. Herds of people cluster around the exit to catch His Holiness on the way out. A man and woman from the Indian sangha precede the procession with a bowl of ashes and a stick of burning incense. A middle-aged monk runs down the steps followed by the rifleman. Two monks flank His Holiness on either side, one hand each wrapped in their robe. Like a precious gem they hold His Holiness as he descends.

For many, if not most, attending the teachings is more about seeing the Dalai Lama than hearing his words. His presence lights the path for the doubtful. In title, he's the living embodiment of Chenrezig, the Bodhisattva of compassion, but he's also a humble human whose presence clearly shows that a life of infinite compassion and truth can be realized by all, grounding abstract Buddhist teachings into reality.

TAKING REFUGE IN SERVICE
An American doctor committed to the principles of seva—selfless service—assists Tibetan refugees in India

A YOUNG WOMAN stands inside the kitchen of her small mud-brick home in a Tibetan refugee camp in Ladakh, India.

"She's scared," the nurse translates to Dr. Cary Rasof, who has just diagnosed the woman's mother with Hepatitis B.

"But your mother is old," Rasof replies, trying to calm her down.

The woman relaxes slightly. Indeed, her mother has lived with Hepatitis B, a potentially chronic condition that gradually damages the liver, into old age. Likely, she will too. Either way, she's still fearful after getting the diagnosis—both for herself and her child.

Rasof found himself in this refugee camp by chance. Not tied to an organization or funding, Rasof is an independent volunteer who has committed his life to serving others based on the principles of seva—an Indian term for selfless service. Rasof relies on 17 years of volunteer experience and the connections he's made to get from project to project, and to help fund the testing and treatment for Tibetans with Hepatitis B.

While in Ladakh working on a project to create better health care access for a remote village, he learned of the disproportionately high rate of Hepatitis B among Tibetan refugees, and put together a public awareness program encouraging Tibetans to get tested. After giving 10 presentations, nearly all of the 2,000 in attendance agreed to undergo testing. Of those, approximately 10 percent have been diagnosed with the virus, most unaware they were infected.

Rasof and Sidol, a Tibetan nurse from the nearby city of Leh, walk past a generator sitting at the entrance of the ramshackle clinic. Inside, the nurse-doctor duo pull up chairs around a small table. A medicine cabinet with semi-stocked shelves stands in the corner of the mostly empty room. Next door, a team of nurse assistants hunch over a table with vials of blood laid out on it.

"Out of 800 [patients], 80 have tested positive so far," Sidol informs the doctor, looking down at her files. He nods, knowing the consequences and the importance of getting treatment.

Hepatitis B is a worldwide disease. According to the World Health Organization, the virus has infected approximately two billion people and 350 million suffer chronically, causing an estimated 600,000 deaths per year.

The disease is most prevalent in Asia and the Pacific islands, accounting for 78 percent of those chronically infected in the world. The highly infectious virus spreads through childbirth, blood transfusions and sexual transmission.

In the Tibetans' case, it's most often transmitted through birth. Some who contract the disease cannot completely fight it off, leading to an increased risk of liver damage, cirrhosis of the liver and liver cancer. Though for many, including most of the refugees, the disease lies dormant, allowing them to conduct relatively normal lives.

Signalling the end of the day, the refugee camp's driver pulls up in his dust-caked jeep designed for the rough Ladakhi terrain. Rasof and the all-women medical team pile into the vehicle to get a lift back to the main clinic. The jeep drives past a large metal sign that says, "IMMUNIZE. Miss not a single child" before stopping at a slightly larger, better maintained clinic.

Rasof walks into the office of Karma Gendun, the Executive Secretary for the Tibetan Primary Health Centre, and pulls out his laptop. He types up a medical report form for their staff to use as a template, paying close attention to its proper formatting.

Rasof has to feel comfortable dealing with bureaucracy in order to be effective in his work. He will sometimes approach the regional medical authority to discuss his plans and register his project. To more effectively handle this small project, however, he chose to involve as few people as possible.

"I would recommend staying subtle and under the radar because once politicians are involved there is confusion," Rasof says. "We are for the people and keep it that way."

Gendun walks in and takes a seat behind his desk. The two discuss treatment options and costs. The conversation turns to specific cases as Gendun pulls out a sheet with the names of patients who have been treated with traditional Tibetan medicine.

Though it's too early to definitively prove how many have been cured, his figures show that 30 per cent no longer show signs of the disease. The results demonstrate that the treatment is a potentially effective and safe option without the side effects of conventional drugs.

The Tibetan treatment is a hopeful sign for the community. It's a local solution to a global problem, and just the kind of solution Rasof likes to see. He got into this line of work to create seva opportunities for others. As more Tibetans get tested and seek treatment, more Tibetan doctors get to help their own people.

"Personal and global transformation comes from being of service to others," Rasof says. "It is through this notion of loving and giving that we change and grow and improve ourselves and our world."

INTERNET WOES

The challenge of getting online in India

THE LOCATION IS LEH, the main city in India's northernmost frontier of Ladakh, the semi-autonomous region within the conflict-ridden Jammu and Kashmir state. Situated high up in the Himalayas at 3,500 m (11,500 ft), the region enjoys isolation from the tumult of India. But what comes with that isolation are power shortages, mountain roads that you can drive 25 kph on (when they're not shut down with snow) and telecommunication challenges so intense they can quickly gray your hair.

I start my workday trying to go to Chillout, my usual Internet spot. An appropriately named shop because "chill" is exactly what you have to be to get anything done around here. The proprietor of the shop, Tenzin, is sitting out front. I see the sliding metal screen door raised from a distance. Good sign. It means he's open, which he's often not because of either a power shortage or Internet shortage.

"No power" he tells me, and he's not going to run the generator because he doesn't get enough customers in the morning to warrant running the generator and hooking up the satellite Internet, which is more expensive than the standard Internet connection which will be down because of the power shortage.

I continue walking down the street to the next choice location that also has satellite. Metal screen door is down. Closed. They don't have their generator going likely for the same reason—not enough business in the morning, so they didn't bother opening up.

My hunt continues. I backtrack 50 m to Get Connected in the bowels of the market. With lime green walls and wood panelling it looks like a retro TV set. Open, but lights are off. A couple of people are seated on their laptops using their battery power. My battery will only last two hours, so I leave, go to the store to buy a few things then walk back. Power's back on. I "get connected," take a seat at the table at the back and plug into the broadband wifi.

I'm surfing for about half an hour when I get an error. Down. I look next to me. A guy stares back. Same deal. It's down he tells me; they're getting a new connection. I see the owner in the corner typing away at his network computer. He then jumps from computer to computer tapping in IP codes and reconnecting the waiting surfers to the grid. He ends with me and gives me the codes… which don't work. I get an error (invalid subnet mask). I figure it's looking for a fourth number so I tell him to type in an extra zero at the end. Success! It worked and once again, I'm back online, albeit at a much slower pace.

I feel like I've walked all day through the desert and my thirst has been quenched with a few drops of water. Despite crawling along at the pace of a circa 1993 modem I have Internet. With Internet out here being down 40 percent of the time, sometimes entire days at a time, sometimes for minutes, I'm just grateful to have something… anything. As long as I'm crawling I'm moving. I don't care.

I work away for a while until the broadband takes a hike. It's approaching North American business hours and I have three interviews set up that I have to do. Looking like I'm not going to be able to Skype I pack up and go to the STD phone (no, not that kind of STD… it actually stands for Subscriber Trunk Dialling), what should be a solid connection, right?

I make my first call. "You're cutting out," my caller says and tells me to call him back in 45 minutes. I make a couple more calls. Same deal, more of the same. Phone and Internet down… now this is a problem.

Broadband is back. I figure even this low "high speed" would be about as bad quality as the STD option so I make the call I'd promised to make. First using Skype to call my friend to test. The call dropped three times. Good thing he's a good friend. Once the broadband cut out completely. Twice I got cut off because the connection was just too slow. It came back on—OK I've got to make this quick I tell him "because I don't know how long it will last."

We rush through a nine-minute-long conversation, making plans to meet in South India in December. OK, now on to an important business call, an interview I've been working on setting up for four days. Ten minutes go by, things are about as smooth as things can be in a slow-high speed scenario. He just phases out a couple of times, then boom, dropped. Broadband is out. He was really busy and was taking his time to talk to me so I was pissed. Trying to salvage whatever I could from this half interview I run over to the STD phone in the cafe. The phone is occupied. I pack up my gear in a hurry and bolt out, looking for the next place to make a call.

I walk across the street to a money changer-cum-Internet café-cum-guy who will lend you his cell phone for a fee (note: in Indian English the word "cum" is commonly used with the standard Oxford dictionary definition: "Combined with, also used as (used to describe things with a dual nature or function)" not the way it's regularly used in North America). The owner passes me his cell and I make my call. Voicemail three times. It appears that all my attempts are foiled this day so I leave a message to do the rest of the interview by email. I go back. Broadband is back and I type up my email and off I go.

Travelling in India has its challenges—to put it mildly. Travellers get used to the challenges and grow from them (and maybe grow a few gray hairs at the same time), but sometimes India travellers *absolutely lose it*.

While hanging out in Internet cafes in Leh I've heard people yell at their computer after it goes down and kills the email they've been working on, get verbally abusive with the owners and just overall bitch and complain. Though my living depends on accessing the Internet for research-based writing, I like to write reflective pieces when I get the chance . And with Ladakh being the reflective place it is, having copious amounts of time to journal is not a bad thing. Sure beats staring at a blank screen half the day

BANGALORE
One foot dangling in the future, one hoof rooted in the past

SADAR PATRAPPA ROAD is commonly abbreviated to S.P. Road, nice and short for those wanting to save some time saying the extra syllables. This is Bangalore after all—the hub of India's fast-paced IT industry, and S.P. is where its tech lovers congregate.

A colourful array of small-box computer and electronic shops sit side-by-side, stacked on top of another, stretching on and on for several city blocks. Signs reading Satyam Computer, Om Electronics and Digitech, compete with one another in a screaming match of salesmanship.

Banners float overhead the width of the narrow road. "Raj Shree Computers – Brand new computer @6999." One Dell banner points to the right. Behind it, another Dell banner points to the left in a confused tangle of conflicting messages.

Guys in their twenties and thirties scurry from shop to shop picking up their gadget of the moment. They wiggle through a maze of motorcycles parked two rows thick as they dart across the narrow street, called by one sign or another to their tech-gods. They wear either the colonial-influenced western attire of polyester slacks and short-sleeved shirt or the more recent westernization: blue jeans and t-shirt.

The local temple, a little streetsider for regular pujas, doesn't get much traffic. Despite the frenetic buzz of activity in every direction, it sits lonely during the middle of this workday. Around it, a few street vendors sell some snacks—not a restaurant in sight. The watermelon woman sits behind a cart with neatly lined up bright slices of red fruit, no customers. The coconut man with his mobile shop, an Indian bike with coconuts hanging evenly on either side of

23

the frame and machete sitting in the front basket, is doing steady business.

But only the truly food hungry slow down to stop for food. The S.P. crowd's thirst is for technology, its hunger is to get wired. When not shopping inside the stores, they're browsing keychain flashlights, motorized toy tanks and other electronic gadgetry sold on the streets.

Two-wheelers (motorcycles and mopeds), three-wheelers (tuk tuks) and the odd four-wheeler (cars) clash along the narrow street, bullying their way through human traffic. With all the competing sounds, their horns don't generate much notice among pedestrians and even less care. It's with mechanical might that these metal noisemaking wheel-boxes prevail.

"Heay. Heaaayy." Amid the multi-wheeler zoo come three wheels and four hooves. A dignified looking chocolate-brown horse wearing a head strap with a tiny bell dangling in front of its forehead is commandeered by a barefoot middle-aged man in a wooden cart, legs folded underneath him as he leans to one side casually making his way through traffic. "Heay. Heaaayy. Heay. Heaaayy," he rhythmically repeats his traffic-clearing mantra to some effect.

The horse and horseman command attention with dignity and grace. With slightly more than their usual road traffic indifference, the crowd seems to quieten just enough for the jingling of the bell to be heard. The pedestrians of S.P. pay attention, opening a path as he plows straight ahead, hauling his long load of aluminum pipes to the mechanical shops at the far end of S.P. Road.

Plowing straight ahead. That's what Bangalore is doing. It's hurtling at the speed of light through the 21st century, yet with one hoof stubbornly dragging "behind" the times. Amid the soundtrack of honking horns and beeping mobile phones, the tapping of horse hooves signal a reminder to past days and serve as a connection to nature. India's strong traditional culture maintains a place for everyone, even barefoot horsemen among the highest of the nation's high-techies.

CHECKMATE
Play the game with mindfulness and equanimity

A STRAY COW is walking toward me. I cross the street to give it space, careful to avoid stepping on a tail of one of the many sprawled out, potentially rabid, dogs that lay on the other side. Honk. I turn to see a car driving behind the cluster of people I'm walking among. We're too far out in the middle of the narrow road for the car to pass, so we squish oh so close to the indiscernible cow-munched trash and liquid-lined gutter.

Another honk, this time totally unnecessary, just a byproduct of Indian drivers having grown accustomed to honking their horns. The honk serves as a reminder to come back to the present moment, as Vietnamese monk Thich Nhat Hanh would call a "bell of mindfulness." Good thing too, since straight ahead of me lies a veritable minefield of shit. A fecal collection of strays for me to scatalogue — a cow pat here, some donkey scat over there, dog poop scattered all around.

Breathing in, I smell cow dung, breathing out, I smile at the cow dung — I'm reminded of a mindfulness gatha of Nhat Hanh's that teaches us to equanimously appreciate the "bad" with the "good." Walking along I feel a splatter across my chest. I look up to see a construction worker three stories up splashing mortar on the wall. I'm thankful. It could have been a lot worse. Farther down the road I spot a sidewalk, a rare sight. I enter the crowded market, guarding my wallet as I walk.

The checklist of items to be aware of while walking the streets of India is exhaustive. Off-street brings a host of different problems: watching what food can safely be eaten, getting ripped off,

25

contracting malaria, developing altitude sickness, the list goes on. India hands out these regular reminders as presents for us to use as we choose. As bells of mindfulness, we can see them as opportunities to constantly be aware of each others' presence or we can get exhausted from living in constant worry. The first choice is to live in the present moment, the second to live in the future.

Fear is simply a working of the mind based on future-oriented thought — we can control it as long as we are conscious of it. India is a fine place to put this perception of fear to the test since the regularity of present moment reminders provides consistent practice. Travelers to India tend to love or hate the country. It's even more common to swing back and forth between loving and hating it while on the trip. But, it's not that the country is "good" or "bad." How the outcome is determined, like everything in life, depends solely on our perception.

Equanimity, the acceptance of everything without avoiding the "bad" and desiring the "good," is easily practiced in India. Lack of choice is one reason. After all, if we can only get one type of chocolate bar, we might as well be happy with it because the alternative is nothing. Second, questioning everything that happens on a daily basis would be pointless since there wouldn't be much room left to actually live a life between all the fearful thoughts. In Indian cities, it's possible to walk down a street and get asked by shopkeepers every few steps you take to buy their goods. If we had an opinion about what is "good" and "bad" about the sheer volume of interactions and potential mishaps that happen on a daily basis in India, we would live in unhappiness. There are just so many opportunities in India to practice equanimity we might as well practice it, otherwise end up in the "good" and "bad" trap.

India does have its share of problems, but as usually happens in our fear-obsessed world, what we perceive and what is reality are worlds apart. With a resident population of 1.2 Billion and a large tourist population adding to that, the proportion of incidents isn't really as high as it seems. Some issues are real and need to be avoided, but most are made-up wanderings of the fanciful mind.

Equanimity neutralizes fear. With billions of people living on Earth, problems happen. That will never change. What can change is our response. We determine whether an event is to be feared or if it just an event. If something "bad" happens, the choice is ours to label it as "bad" and then live in fear of it happening again or we can drop the label and just see it as an event that happened. The more difficult the outcome, the harder it is to deal with, but the larger the lesson we need to learn.

On the rare occasion, even when going with the flow of equanimity, we can get hurt. It could be that we thought we were in the flow, but unconsciously were not. Or it could have been a result of our karmic conditioning from the present or a past life. There's no sense questioning it. Equanimity can be our greatest ally in determining the truth of a situation. It helps us accept what has happened and move on in the present moment, rather than being frozen in the future.

As Buddhists speak of equanimity, eventually everything becomes just an event, not to be liked or disliked. Losing our attachment to fear helps us abide in that place of peace. A place where every event is pure joy.

Just like a master of chess plays the game with strategy rather than passively reacting to an opponent's every move, as masters of life, we can play the game with a strategy of mindfulness and equanimity to act in the world rather than react to events with desire and aversion. In this way, life cannot lead us along in a game that we do not control. In fact, the game never even began. We called checkmate from the very start.

BORDER WALK

The tense Indo-Pak border is opening up to a brand of tourism that's unexpectedly calm

WHAM. I JUST landed a foot-high bounce off the back seat of the bus. I'm on a 10-hour coccyx-crunching ride that winds up and up and up what's disputedly called the highest motorable pass in the world—Khardungla—with magnificent views of Leh valley below. The 18,300 foot rollercoaster of a ride is a trip in itself. On its way through barren desert and high mountain passes, the bus stops at four military checkpoints along the carefully controlled Pakistan border in India's northernmost Jammu and Kashmir state, ending in the green oasis of Turtuk.

"One photo, one photo," I hear in surround sound as I stroll the narrow stone footpaths of Turtuk. Two Baltistani girls dressed in colourful traditional dresses, baggy pants and matching headscarves follow me, asking for their picture to be taken yet again.

I look up to see five more young girls smiling down at me from their rooftop, all asking for "one photo." Snap. I capture all seven of them, show the picture in the viewfinder and continue walking down the path until a minute later I yet again hear the familiar "one photo" mantra.

It's not vanity driving the villagers of Turtuk to seek photographs, but a curiosity of tourists and a desire for cultural interaction. Butted up against what's considered one of the most dangerous borders in the world, the Pakistan border in India's northernmost state of Jammu and Kashmir, the mainly Muslim agrarian village used to be part of Pakistan (more specifically the region of Baltistan) prior to the 1971 Indo-Pak war and just recently opened to tourism in 2010.

A trip to Turtuk is a trip back to a simpler time when people were more connected to nature. It seems everywhere I walk in the village a cleverly diverted irrigation stream gurgles alongside me, while a food forest of bountiful apricot and apple trees shade villagers with their low-hanging branches heavy with produce. Rather than getting cut down, trees are integrated into the building of homes. Streamlets pass right through the middle of people's homes, powering their mills and providing easy access to fresh water.

A wave of relaxation melts the stress soon after arriving due in part to the slow pace of village life and in part to the village's close integration with nature.

As I walked and walked through the fields I couldn't help but think how being here is like village therapy. A walk back to a simpler time, to a time when the important things were the focus of one's life: nature, community, real food, fresh air.

Being immersed in that environment, even though just for a few days, had such a calming effect that it brought me to the point where the mind dropped its story. It just had no more ammunition to divert itself. I saw with my own eyes how much sense living this way makes and how far off the mark our industrialized society has gone.

Turtuk's calm nature stands in stark contrast to its heavily-fortified surroundings. While walking through the outskirts of the village, two military officers patrolling the border stopped me from walking any further along the valley leading to Pakistan. But they were chill about it. They gave me a *bidi* (Indian cigarette) and we exchanged a few words. Like the relaxed border checkpoints along the way these people in uniform did not express the charge that can come with wearing the uniform. Living among that environment I can see why they're so chill.

With an army of 1.1 million, the tension felt from India's military might is ever present, spicing the general calmness of a trip to

Turtuk with the occasional tense moment. Yet given the political and military charge this border has, I'd rarely felt calmer in my life.

The few visitors to the village consistently comment that they just feel different when spending time in the village. Village therapy is such a simple thing—bring ourselves back to simplicity to come to peace and realize our truth.

THIKSEY MONASTERY

Ladakh offers respite from India's busyness

FIFTY MONKS SIT cross-legged in long rows. Their prayer books, narrow strips of thick paper bound by string, sit open in front of them. They chant the Buddhist sutras to a hypnotic single drumbeat while occasional horn blasts pierce the air. A picture of the Dalai Lama sits front-centre in Thiksey Monastery's prayer hall. Colourful wall murals and thangka paintings fill the room with Mahayana Buddhism's extensive pantheon of deities. I sit at the back absorbing the trance-like ambiance as the rising sun slowly lights up the room.

Unlike most monasteries, Thiksey invites tourists to take part in their morning ritual. Tourists can even stay in their guesthouse located right on top of their piece of hilltop paradise in India's northernmost region of Ladakh.

At the end of the ceremony, young monks attend to their puja duties. A couple of mini-monks speedily zip around the room sweeping the floor. A couple more walk around with steel pitchers serving a drink. Holy water of some sort or other I reckon. Or so I convince myself as I gingerly accept the cup. Looks like water with some spices added to it. I sip with hesitation, eventually drinking it all figuring that if it came from this holy place it can't make me sick.

I shift my focus to a Bhavacakra painting at the entrance as I leave. The Wheel of Life symbolizes the cyclic nature of samsara—the continuous cycle of life and death. A pig, bird, and snake chase each other in the wheel's nucleus, signifying ignorance, attachment, and aversion, the roots of all suffering according to Buddhists.

Like a bird, I flutter off in search of something else to look at in this expansive monastery. My desires land me smack in front of a

33

49-foot Maitreya Buddha statue, the future Buddha. I stand in awe, gazing at its sublime beauty. An intricately detailed headdress adorns the top of the Buddha's head. His gold-painted face radiates peace. As one of Ladakh's most photographed Buddha statues, the room is dotted with signs alerting visitors not to take a picture of oneself with the Buddha. Pictures of the Buddha alone are OK. Anyway, since the Maitreya Buddha represents the future Buddha within us all, when we take a picture of it, we're symbolically taking a picture of ourselves.

I meander through the remaining meditation halls on the lower levels before finding my way to the roof. The 360-degree mountain view keeps me there for some time. And despite being midday, Ladakh's 11,000-foot altitude and desert climate produces comfortably dry heat, even in the summer, making it an ideal getaway for the Indian traveler wanting to escape the choking heat and monsoon rains of lowland India. Snowy Stok range holds my gaze the longest. Like a formidable sentry, the wall of mountains forms the southern ridge to Indus valley, the main population belt in Ladakh.

Ladakh is as empty as Delhi is full. The whole region only has about 200,000 people and the "big" city of Leh has a mere 30,000, which along with the large tourist population is still enough to cause the busy streets, honking horns, and chest-constricting pollution common to Indian cities, making a side trip to Thiksey that much better. Just a short drive from Leh, it's a getaway that provides the same kind of peace and solitude that the monks get to live in, but without having to climb deep into the Himalayas to get it.

I duck through a tiny doorway to have a look at the dark, little library that houses a number of thick volumes, including the Kangyur and Stangyur sacred texts, before heading to the stupa platform.

One of the monastery's older monks slowly circumambulates the platform, prayer beads in hand, deep in meditation. Seven simple stupas—Buddhist shrines containing sacred relics—are lined up in a row like sentries overlooking the farmers' fields below. Despite the grandeur of the monastery's halls, it is this platform that attracts me most. This nature hall overlooking the deep green Indus valley, butted up against the barren, brown Himalayan rock is like a window to nature.

A farmer calls out commands to his zos, a yak-cow crossbreed, to plough his field. Slowly it chugs along. First one direction, then the other, and back again. For centuries these monks have been looking down at the movement of villagers below while walking in circles and chanting in repetition. The monastic presence seems to have some kind of effect on the villagers. The pace of village life is so slow. They are still living much like their ancestors did centuries ago.

The zos slowly continues along its circular path. The farmer keeps on shouting the same commands like a mantra. The "Om mani padme hum" chant cycles through my mind in repetition as I sit on the platform staring down at the village, entranced by peace.

SUSTAINABILITY AS SPIRITUAL PRACTICE

Volunteer at Sadhana Forest to learn how to live sustainably

IT'S A PLEASANTLY warm evening in the south of India. A group of about one hundred people, mostly in their 20s and 30s, are gathered inside Sadhana Forest's main building watching Plastic Planet, a documentary about the plastic industry and the effect plastic has on the environment. Looking around I don't see much plastic at all. The structure is made of bamboo held together by twine. The roof, thatched leaves. Natural fibre carpets line the floors, some wooden children's toys lie in the corner. Aside from the screen, the player and the odd little thing here and there, this community really does stay plastic-free, an amazing feat in this "plastic planet" of ours. It's one way Sadhana Forest truly practices what it preaches.

Sadhana Forest is a community within a community—Auroville, an intentional community that started in 1968, inspired by the teachings of the great Indian sage Sri Aurobindo, hence the name Auroville. Among intentional communities—groups of like-minded people living together for a common purpose—Auroville is massive at 2300 people. The internationally-recognized township within India's Tamil Nadu state is comprised of people from 46 different nations living within smaller communities such as Sadhana Forest.

Arivam Rozin, co-founder of Sadhana Forest, leads the tour. Though he's a few years past his youth, he speaks with the highly-charged intensity of a university student excited at just having discovered an alternative way of life. "The community's four guiding principles are "Veganism/nonviolence, gift economy, inclusivity/diversity, technical sustainable living," he raps out with a consistency that comes from having spoken that line hundreds of times, but with the same enthusiasm as if he was saying it for the first time.

The previous video that had been playing on this community tour and movie night was *Vegan*, a documentary about the effect of meat consumption on the environment and veganism as a viable alternative. As I delight in eating a yummy rice and nut main dish with sweet potato and salad on the side, here again I find that the community indeed remains true to its ideals.

Sadhana Forest's pledge towards veganism furthers their commitment towards sustainability. As the documentary had pointed out, going vegan is the easiest and best thing anyone can do to improve the environment since it reduces the need to cut down countless acres of forest needed to grow food for animals that end up polluting the air with their toxic bodily emissions. Saving forests is something close to Rozin's heart.

In addition to living sustainably and acting as a role model for visitors, Sadhana Forest's daily work is focused on reforestation. Pre-19th century Auroville land was desert. Poor stewardship by the colonial powers resulted in major deforestation and soil erosion problems. "Fifteen minutes after monsoon rains the soil would be dry," Rozin said, explaining the dire erosion issue they faced when first working the land eight years ago.

Rozin leads the large group on a tour of the land. We walk past energy-efficient rocket stoves in the communal kitchen and human electricity generators, recumbent exercise bikes hooked up to a generator, on our way to Challenge Hill, the site of the community's greatest reforestation challenge. "We've done all kinds of crazy stuff," he says, "but weren't able to get survival rates of more than 50 or 60 percent." Rather than soaking into the Earth and replenishing underground water aquifers, rainfall would just fall onto the land and seep into the nearby ocean without adding moisture to the soil, making it a horrendous environment to grow trees.

But displaying true grit common to Aurovillians, the community saw the challenge as an opportunity to improve. "If you can grow on Challenge Hill, you can grow anywhere," Rozin explains, pointing out the benefit to the difficulty.

They've dug 25 kilometers of bunds—long and narrow trenches that facilitate the absorption of water into underground aquifers—throughout the property; built a series of eight dams; and instituted other innovative land stewardship and growing practices to provide a healthy environment for the 26,000 trees they've planted. And their planting efforts don't stop in Auroville. They do reforestation work in other parts of India and have a large project going in one of Haiti's poorest parts.

Gift economy is another community principle, which is in practice on this night. I had seen a poster advertising this event offering a free movie, tour and dinner. They had even organized free buses to transport the 100-plus attendees from Auroville's town center. They accept donations, but I didn't hear them ask for a single rupee. "How do you get funding?" a visitor asks Rozin the obvious question. The community survives on small donations and voluntary simplicity. Free food and accommodation is offered to anyone who wants to volunteer, he says. The gift economy works on the basis of generosity. Give and the universe will provide. They've been going eight years and expanding, so it's a practice that's working for them.

Sadhana Forest has no shortage of volunteers. People from around the world flock to Sadhana for varying amounts of time, filling it to a population as high as 120. Of those there's a core group of about 10 long-term volunteers, the rest are short-term.

"I thrive on this diversity. So many abilities to give, share ideas," Rozin says of the community's final principle, inclusivity/diversity. He's proud of Sadhana Forest's lack of institutionalization. His children don't go to school, but learn from the community. Old people come and get taken care of rather than get sent off to old age homes. People with severe mental problems are taken in. If anyone wants to come to Sadhana Forest, they can come. No one is left behind. It's a challenge Rozin asserts, but it's worth it.

Looking around, the crowd is not actually all that diverse. Mostly young white Westerners, but that's a common sight among India travelers in general, perhaps making the desire for inclusivity and diversity that much stronger.

Sadhana means spiritual practice in Sanskrit. Practicing these four principles are actions just as important to the community as its reforestation work. If a few less trees are planted because problems come up within the community, that's fine. To live sustainably and in harmony can be challenging. It's why so many duck out and settle for a somewhat eco-friendly lifestyle and a smidgeon of contentedness. Rozin and others living at Sadhana Forest realize the importance of this work and act as a much-needed model of true sustainable living. A model that anyone can come visit, learn from and call their home.

OM ARUNACHALA

Tiruvannamalai—a pilgrimage place for millions

FOR A CITY of only 150,000, Tiruvannamalai sure has a lot of people. It's not the citizens mind you, but the visitors that make this small city in Tamil Nadu, India so crowded. Hindus visit by the millions for pilgrimages and foreigners come for the many ashrams. Both crowd the city with the intention of spirituality on their mind.

Sacred Mount Arunachala rises from an otherwise flat terrain high into the sky. This auspicious mountain is the main attraction for Hindu pilgrims. Every full moon hundreds of thousands walk barefoot around it along the 14-km girivalam route. Those numbers swell from a few hundred thousand on a regular month to a few million for Deepam, the festival of lamps which happens in November or December. For this particular festival, a massive ghee-fuelled lamp is lit on the top of the mountain that can be seen for miles.

Though Arunachala is the centrepiece of attraction, the temple is the actual hub of worship. With tall spires that stand high in the sky, Tiru's intimidating Shiva temple spans several blocks in the centre of the city. The temple is actually a complex of smaller temples housed within its ornately crafted walls complete with statues, a pond and the occasional elephant.

Tiru has been pulling pilgrims in for centuries, a number of whom ended up sticking around and setting up their ashrams. One of these, Ramana Maharshi, a sage known for his clear teachings of Vedanta, had drawn pilgrims to Tiru from around the world during his lifetime and continues to draw visitors in to the large ashram.

A short rickshaw ride from the Shiva temple is the ashram area. Ramana's ashram draws the largest chunk of pilgrims, both Indian and Western. But Ramana's is far from the only ashram in Tiru. Every couple of blocks there's an ashram. Larger ones like Yogi Ramsuratkumar's ashram are hard to miss for the landmark they set in a town that's hard to navigate. Others, such as Siva Sakhti's barely stand out from the wall of buildings that it is a part of—an unobtrusive sign indicating darshan at 10:00 a.m. the only visible signal that it is an ashram.

Seekers from around the world flock to, and migrate to, Tiru. Rental homes are abundant, but get rented fast in the busy months, particularly in January and February. Many travellers to Tiru end up settling in for months at a time to take in the teachings of their favourite guru, or a sampling of them all. And they aren't all Indian teachers. With the many Western visitors come Western teachers like Mooji and James Swartz.

Tiru's spiritual universe extends beyond gurus and ashrams as it's filled with yoga centres, kirtan gatherings (call and response to Indian sacred music) and conscious dance events, making it an easy place for spiritual travellers in India to settle in and stay for a while. Despite there being a lot to do it is the regular community of people that come back year after year and live there that make Tiru one of those truly special places for travellers where they can easily feel at home.

KALARIPAYATTU

Experience the awesome acrobatics of this ancient martial art

KERALA IN SOUTHWESTERN India is known for its vibrant arts scene, in part because of the ancient martial art Kalaripayattu, known as one of the oldest martial arts, if not the oldest, which originated in this part of India.

Kalaripayattu is marked by high-flying acrobatics, fluid movements and weaponry. With lithe bodies, Kalaripayattu artists mimic the flowing movements of animals local to South India such as the tiger, elephant and snake.

Legends trace this mother of all martial arts back through early Hindu mythology to Sage Parasurama, known as one of the seven immortal humans in Hindu culture. More recently, in the 11th or 12th century AD it was first documented as being used in the war between the Chera and Chola dynasties in South India.

Attacks in this martial art include kicking, grappling and striking, both with weapons and without. The high jumps, leaps and graceful movements of kalaripayattu have predictably caught the attention of Bollywood, with the art form being incorporated into movies like *Asoka*, *Lajja* and even into Jackie Chan's movie *The Myth*.

Beyond the lethal blows delivered by swords and sticks, warriors practicing kalaripayattu could knock out or even kill their enemies just by hitting specific marmam points on the body, which are the same vital points that form the basis of India's ancient healing system, Ayurveda. Because of this advanced knowledge, kalaripayattu practitioners were also skilled in traditional medicine and massage, which was a necessary skill to learn when getting banged up so badly in combat or even just while training.

"Kalari" means school or gymnasium in the local Malayalam language of Kerala. "Payattu" means to fight or exercise. The martial art is embedded in the history of the region with these fight schools churning out warriors who would use the martial art to defend the king and kingdom.

The British banned kalaripayattu for fear of rebellion and anti-colonial sentiment, no doubt fearing its effectiveness. But it then went underground, resurfacing in the 1920s as part of a rediscovery of traditional arts in South India.

For travellers wanting to check out Kerala's arts scene, Fort Kochi (also spelled "Fort Cochin") offers a variety of entertainment options. Here there's no problem finding kalaripayattu performances, which are not as common as the more widespread kathakali dances. The Kerala Kathakali Centre is one such place that offers daily performances in kalaripayattu as well as kathakali and Indian classical music and dance.

SHIKARA HO!

Hop aboard for a look at the life of Dal Lake's boat hawkers

FROM THE STERN, Mr. Nice spots three elderly Western women out on a day tour of Dal Lake. He promptly spins his 20' wooden shikara in a 180° to aim in that direction, then paddles alongside. His partner and best friend, Mr. Bhat, greets the ladies, then jumps straight into the sales pitch. "Would you like some silver?" he asks, handing a necklace to one of them. The pitches continue as Nice paddles methodically alongside.

"They never stop," one of the women sighs in a thick Danish accent. Out of politeness, the woman closest feigns interest by taking a look at the jewellery held out to her. "I can assure you that you won't be selling anything to us," she affirms. The sales attempts continue for a few minutes until Bhat realizes he's wasting his time. "Thank you, have a nice evening," he says. Then motions to Nice to pull away.

Bhat and Nice are among 150 floating salesmen who hawk their wares on Srinigar's Dal Lake in Kashmir, India. Their brightly-painted canoe-like boats called shikaras serve as their moving sales centers. They pursue tourists being paddled around in shikara-taxis or hop right up onto their houseboats. It's a 24-hour hustle. The flotilla sales approach offends some; low prices and quality products entice others.

Nice and Bhat (actually pronounced "butt") are lifelong friends who grew up on Dal Lake. Both left Kashmir at a young age during the war with Pakistan—the Indian army was killing off Kashmiri youth under the suspicion of them being terrorists. They both

45

worked at bricks-and-mortar jewelry shops across India for a few years. When tensions eased in Kashmir, they returned to their homes and converted their stationary trade into a mobile one. The choice was easy—stay confined within four walls or paddle around on the beautiful waters of Dal Lake. Like others in the community, they grew up paddling from a young age. For them it's just back to the lake life routine.

Jewellery isn't all that's sold on Dal Lake. Hawkers are neatly divided into camps: jewellery, carvings, pashmina/clothing, paper mache, flowers, and food. Though they all know each other and generally get along, they stick to their groups just like on a grade school playground.

Selling season on the lake runs from May to November. Come winter the salesmen rest their weary bodies and turn to the fine movements of jewellery crafting. They make necklaces, rings, pendants, or anything they feel a tourist might want. To keep costs low, the two buy rocks in bulk sizes then cut them down to size. They sell the full range of gems from around the world, but offer the best deals on sapphires and turquoise, both stones native to Kashmir. From their warehouse home they pack their goods into several metal briefcases, allowing for perfect portability between the boat and the tourists' houseboat docks.

Nice turns around and paddles back to the "highway"—a wide stretch of relatively weed-free water that leads to the market. In the market, paddlers can maneuver their shikaras up to paddle-through shops where they can get anything from fruit to fast food. Don't want to get out of the boat? No problem. Shopkeepers have mastered the toss, making the floating shopping experience a quick and fluid one.

The two in the baby-blue shikara paddle past Razat, the benevolent boss of the shikara salesmen union, who flashes a smile and gives a double-thumbs up from the cabin of his shikara as they pass. All 150 salesmen on the lake are licensed with the Kashmir government. The hawking licenses help keep the trade reputable and the union provides a point of contact for tourists who get ripped off or harassed.

Their lives are intimately tied to selling on the water. The shikara salesmen paddle all day, all week, taking breaks with their groups for lunch and tea. They design the boats for their lives in them. On Nice's shikara, shoes come off at the bow before walking into the brown, carpet-lined cabin. Two small speakers point into the cabin from the front. To complete the surround sound, two more hide neatly tucked away behind the seat along with a small amplifier and battery supply. A single CFL lights up the cabin at night. Simple, but homely for an oversized canoe designed for a lifetime on the lake.

Boat hawking is as much a lifestyle as a job. Paddling around on the lake amidst abundant bird life comes serene benefits, and connects the sellers to their environment. But aggressive competition with other hawkers for just a few sales a day gets tiring. The routine isn't an easy one. Long days of paddling make for a real physical workout. But it's the financial aspect of the job that causes the most stress. They have seven months to make a salary large enough to support a family for a year. Though foreign tourists can sometimes spend $100 to $200 on a purchase, the sizeable Indian tourist population rarely spends more than a few bucks.

The routine inevitably causes friction with some tourists—not everyone enjoys interruption on a romantic sunset paddle. But, the shikara salesmen don't see their aggressive sales approach as unusual. It's just the way it is. The way it has to be.

"Mr. Nice" was bestowed the name for his kindness. He goes out of his way to help direct lost tourists paddling around the labyrinthine waters of Dal Lake. Since the tight competition demands salesmen draw on whatever tools of economic survival they have, his niceness also serves another purpose. He's not just another aggressive salesman; he's a friend on the lake, with something to sell.

3 PEACOCKS & A MONKEY

Meeting sattva and rajas at Ramana's ashram

I STARED AT the jet-black statue of Ramana for a long time. Locking eyes with the *jnani*, I felt his presence in the ashram, inside me. The near-perfect life-sized rendering of the wise sage, hunched over in sitting position, had an aliveness, a realness that made his presence palpable despite his passing more than 60 years ago.

After spending many years living in caves on Mount Arunachala, Ramana Maharshi settled into his ashram in Tiruvannamalai, India where he remained a fixture as solid as the stone statue that now depicts his bodily form. There he taught scores of seekers who journeyed from around the world to learn something of awareness by sitting with this living embodiment of the Self.

When Ramana was dying of cancer, his disciples expressed their concern at his imminent loss. "I am not going anywhere, where shall I go?" he responded. "I shall be there where I am always."

So, having deep respect for Ramana, I wondered whether it was just me feeling his presence.

Two days later I returned to the ashram. But this time it was neither Ramana's presence nor the inviting temple filled with peaceful meditators that caught my attention. Above the temple, two peacocks stood in graceful stillness atop the two corners and a third above the front entrance. All three faced outward like gargoyles standing sentry over the place.

I stood in awe looking up at the graceful birds for quite some time. They just stood there in silent stillness, in perfect peace. Like satellite dishes they absorbed the treasure of consciousness sitting under their feet and radiated it to all those around.

Visitors to the ashram stopped to gaze at these magnificent birds while locals, accustomed to seeing them regularly, looked up and smiled every now and then.

Just about every time I visited the ashram I saw at least one. Yet, of the six weeks I was in Tiru, I didn't see a single peacock elsewhere in town. It's no coincidence they made their home at the ashram. It seems they're as connected to their inward beauty as people are attracted to their outward beauty.

A week later I returned to the ashram, but with a different intention. I didn't show up to just be. Rather, I went with an agenda: stop in for a short bit of walking meditation during the evening *puja* before making my way to dinner.

Carrying two grocery bags–one cloth, one plastic—I walked through the ashram gate and headed for the temple. A 400-year-old Iluppai tree stood firmly rooted as a living monument just in front of the entrance. Underneath it, a monkey was standing oddly still, leaning over to one side with its eyes intently fixed on me. I felt a strange apprehension, but since I'd never had problems with a monkey before I didn't think anything of it and continued walking.

It lunged at me and grabbed the plastic bag, tearing a hole in it. The contents spilled out onto the ground and within seconds it rummaged through the bottles and snatched the one thing it could eat—a mango bar.

"Damn monkey. Stop!" I yelled, but within seconds, it bolted up the tree.

As I collected my goods from the ground, I felt the stares of the silent piercing into me for breaking their carefully cultivated ashramitic peace and then realized the ridiculousness of the situation.

I got mugged by a monkey. And of all places—at Ramana's ashram, one of the holiest sites in all of Mother India. I'd never been robbed in India until that incident. I felt violated. Though I thought I got violated by a monkey, as always, it was just my mind that I let violate me.

According to the ancient Indian Vedic texts, we have three general qualities of character. *Rajas* is when we're outward focused and over-active, *Tamas* is when we're lethargic and suffering from inertia and, the least common, *sattva* when we're connected to our pure, serene nature. When connected to *sattva*, I saw peacocks. When tempted by *rajas*, I got mugged by a monkey.

I yelled at the monkey to stop, and it did—10 metres above me where it sat on a thick branch, munching away at the bar of sugary goodness.

I looked up at it. It looked down at me. Ridiculous. I started laughing at myself and continued laughing as I walked towards the temple. Here was Ramana staring down at me. It takes a monkey to see a monkey. It takes awareness to see awareness... to be awareness.

SPIRITUAL WARRIORS

Mahabodhi grooms tomorrow's spiritual leaders

"ATTENTION. AT EASE. HATS OFF," a teenage girl shouts orders in her school's courtyard, which until a moment ago was filled with child's laughter and innocent play. Children from six to sixteen quickly form into neat rows. Silence descends on the courtyard, palpably transforming the energy into that of a military camp. Older students pace back and forth, lightly slapping the heads of those who fall out of sync with the precise order. What were once four hundred individuals have quickly converted into a cohesive unit.

Nestled deep in the Indian Himalayas of Ladakh, Mahabodhi is an expansive spiritual community that includes a residential school, home for the aged, monastery, nunnery, and traveller's guesthouse. Founded by Buddhist monk Ven. Bhikkhu Sanghasena, Mahabodhi provides Buddhist spiritual education to more than 400 poor children from surrounding villages who otherwise wouldn't have had access to much of an education. The organization's method of engaged schooling produces students who are spiritually connected, disciplined, and eager to learn.

Vimalachitta, a 15-year-old novice monk, is one of the 400 gathered in the courtyard. He has tentatively chosen the path of a monk, but still has five years to decide before fully committing to the monastic path. "There was an application and selection process for obtaining monkhood when I was nine years old. I passed and got to wear the robes," he proudly exclaims with a big smile when asked why he chose the monastic life. Though he's still figuring out what life as a monk is all about, his strong will is evident. Given that most of his classmates are not following the monastic path, and as such don't have as many strict rules to follow, making the choice he did, and sticking to it, isn't easy.

Konchokdolma, a 10th grade female student spent six years in a military school before transferring to Mahabodhi. When asked if she wants to become a nun, she replies, "Not yet, sir. I believe pureness of heart and happiness is also obtainable without going into nunhood." She dreams about having her own travel agency to work with the many tourists that visit Ladakh. Though the two have very different backgrounds, they share an eagerness to learn, abundant joy, and gratitude to Mahabodhi for the opportunities that they've been given.

A few boys in the Tibetan language class are laughing and acting out. Other students, particularly the monks and nuns, temper the ruckus with their disciplined attention. Tsering, a native Tibetan teaching this class, shows no sign of asserting his authority. Instead, he allows them their moments of glory while converting the energy into his teaching. He walks confidently around the classroom, counting his fingers forcefully in an effort to explain Tibetan grammar. The classroom becomes alive with engaged students following his lead in a spirit of participation that drowns out the troublemakers.

Dharma and discipline come together in a profound way at Mahabodhi. Students maintain strict extra-curricular schedules that start at 5 a.m. and include daily meditation—even for children as young as six—housekeeping chores, homework, and exercise. That disciplined structure helps them to meditate and to form strong, concentrated, and flexible minds.

Anu, a student at Mahabodhi's Institute for the Blind, hangs out in her room after school to diligently complete her homework.

Behind her, three blankets sit neatly folded in an accordion shape at the head of the bed. Two stacks of notebooks are lined up on the dresser beside her and a string of origami lotus flowers surround a hand-drawn Buddha picture on the wall behind. A volunteer dictates her day's homework to her as she punches impressions into a sheet of paper from right to left using her 27 row-by-30 column red plastic slate. Neither her textbook for this civics course nor the texts for many of her other courses are in Braille so she, and the other five blind students, rely on others to dictate to them, putting in the extra work necessary to succeed.

The Mahabodhi community gathers on Sundays for their almost weekly puja, a devotional Buddhist service. For some students in the community, puja is their favorite part of the week. Unfortunately, it doesn't happen as regularly as some would like because the community sometimes loses sight of itself as it gets caught up in the busyness of everyday life.

Rows of monks and nuns as young as six sit cross-legged on the floor at the front of the puja hall. Behind them, students from the boys and girls hostels are neatly lined up, girls on the right, boys on the left. A few elderly residents sit leaned up against the right wall with some travelers scattered throughout the middle. At the front sits Ven. Bhikkhu Sanghasena, who leads the community through the recitation of the <u>five precepts</u>, the basic moral code for Buddhists that teaches nonviolence, right speech, and advises against stealing, sexual misconduct, and the use of intoxicants. "Only universal love and compassion can bring peace, not bombs and guns," he says explaining the importance of adhering to the precepts. "If you violate the last one, you will violate all five," he ends, stressing the need to abstain from intoxicants.

The service proceeds to a short meditation. Even the youngest members of Mahabodhi sit still through the meditation and, more surprisingly, throughout the whole service, which can last as long as four hours. "Sadhu, sadhu, sadhu," the collective chants as they prostrate three times.

Dechen, a teenage girl from the blind hostel takes the stage to sing one of her favorite songs, "Temple of the Holy Buddha." Like most of the songs sung at puja, the theme is spiritual. The meaningful lyrics and strong aura built in the hall create a climate of reverence.

The song embodies what Mahabodhi and its students stand for. A holy home that lies within each of us. The Mahabodhi community is much more than its various buildings and institutions. With regular meditation, dharma lessons, and pujas, the students at Mahabodhi are not likely to forget the spiritual education they've received after graduating. Their disciplined nature has helped them embody the dharma and their eagerness to learn translates to a willingness to try even what is hard, such as adopting a spiritual practice. By creating spiritually engaged, disciplined, and eager students, Mahabodhi is grooming tomorrow's future spiritual leaders.

bhutan

THE LONG ROAD TO HAPPINESS

Is Bhutan really the Shangri-La that people think it is?

"ROAD SINKING, DRIVE SLOWLY" a road sign warns as we drive from the moist and lush lowlands of Bhutan's south border with India to its arid upper reaches in the Himalayas. I ask Tsering, a guide contracted out to show me around the country on a press trip, if that means sinking as in quicksand kind of sinking or the whole ground is sinking. "The whole ground," he answers.

One hour into the country and the adventure has just begun. The population change from India's 1.2 billion to Bhutan's 740,000 is evident the moment I cross the border. The change in roads... not so much.

The windy road carved out of the Himalayan rock had diminished to a muddy mess at this point. Despite being the start of the rainy season, the clouds are just spitting at us on and off. We chug along slowly, squishing our way steadily up. As we pass one road crew after another chipping away with picks and hammers at massive boulders that have slid onto the road, Tsering tells me of the DANTAK, an Indian road building crew who built the roads in Bhutan that opened the country up in the 1960s.

What was just your run-of-the-mill guide remark sounded almost like a joke to me. It's as if the Indian government gifted the Bhutanese a free jalopy with a lifetime warranty that they forced them to service at their own shop—since the Bhutanese have so little labour it creates continued work for the DANTAK to repair the roads they built.

The driver, Lobsang, methodically handles each of the many curves in the road with an ease that makes the drive an overall calming experience despite the unsettling knowledge that the road could disappear underneath us at any point. I study Lobsang next to me with curiosity. He chants mantras under his breath with regularity as he drives. At certain points along the road he puts his hands in a quick Anjali mudra to bow before gripping the wheel again.

I wonder if it's common for drivers in Bhutan to keep the peace like he does. With a speed limit of a whole 50 km on highways and even less on roads this is one country where driving pretty much has to be a practice of mindfulness.

With roads that never seem to go straight for more than a few hundred metres there's ample need to keep attention on the task, and with stunning mountain views there's an equally ample reason to appreciate the natural beauty. The only other alternative would be road rage and with such a low speed limit, meditative drivers and hairpin turns I'd imagine any road ragers in the country would die prematurely of high blood pressure.

Gross National Happiness

IT IS JUST THIS kind of thing that I came to observe in Bhutan. The country captured the world's attention when its fourth king, Jigme Singye Wangchuck, coined the term "Gross National Happiness (GNH)" in 1972 as an alternative measurement of progress in contrast to GDP. And it has managed to keep the world's attention. A few years ago the UN implemented Resolution 65/309, which officially put happiness on the global agenda; several countries have been holding conferences on GNH to figure out how to utilize happiness indicators to make their population happier.

Bhutan's policy on GNH is a four-pillared platform that takes a wholistic look at progress, balancing the non-economic with the economic. The four pillars are good governance, sustainable socio-economic development, cultural preservation and environmental conservation.

Bhutan provides universal healthcare and education to its citizens. Though the services they provide are basic, for one of the least developed countries in the world, providing these services to all their citizens is quite a big accomplishment. They also have a very progressive environmental policy. According to the UNEP, 60 percent of the country will remain forested forever under Bhutanese law. Over 40 percent of their land is protected in the form of national parks, nature preserves and wildlife sanctuaries.

Whether all this talk of Gross National Happiness truly makes a difference is another story. There's a shadow to the happy face people know Bhutan for. Though they provide for the majority of their population in a commendable way, they also booted a sixth of their population, the ethnic Nepali Lhotshampa people, out of the country in what was considered one of the largest ethnic cleansing campaigns in history proportional to population.

Thimphu Touring

ONE BEND AFTER another we climb to a dizzying height of 2,700m before heading back down. The warm moist air and drizzle gives way to cool mountain air and blue skies. I'm now entering the heartland. Thimphu is the capital, a city where a good chunk of the country's population has moved to in recent years in search of urban jobs and a modern lifestyle. A billboard greets me as we enter Thimphu: "Long Live the King."

As I read that I really get the sense of being in an actual kingdom, which to me equates to a more traditional way of life. Thimphu, however, is not the ideal place to start the journey for those looking to experience the traditional Bhutan. Typical of just about any city you get youth sporting funky hairdos and the latest styles. The western influence is very much felt despite a good number of Thimphu folk wearing traditional dress. Building codes in the city demand buildings be constructed according to traditional Bhutanese architecture, but minus the fancy windowsills and door frames and these are concrete behemoths like anywhere else in South Asia. Thimphu is a great place to end a trip to Bhutan though since it has a number of museums and sites that are worth checking out like the impressive 169-foot Buddha statue at Buddha Point.

The statue towers over me with an impressive might. Skill saws buzzing beside me mute some of the awe, making me wonder just how much more impressive this site will be once construction is completed. It feels like a lot of prayer has been done at this site, with a lot more to come: once the Buddha gets finished it'll be a focal point for the city to hold religious events.

The renowned mythologist Joseph Campbell wrote in _The Power of Myth_ that as societies progress, the highest building in a city illustrates what informs the society most. The church was the highest at a time when religion played a dominant role in people's lives. Then government buildings as the state replaced religion as the power brokers in society and finally the skyscrapers of today as corporations dominate our lives. If the Buddha statue is any indication, Bhutan has its priorities pinned on the Buddha as it stands far higher than any other building in Thimphu.

Slow Progress

BHUTAN HAS TAKEN a slow approach to progress. They only allowed tourists to enter the country as recently as 1974, and even then tourists have to spend a minimum of $250 a day during high season ($200 a day during low season), which keeps tourist numbers low since it's considered a large sum for travelling this part of the world. They do this to ensure their policy of high value, low impact tourism, which helps preserve their traditions and culture.

They just became a democracy in 2008, and there too, they've taken a hesitant step. They're still technically a kingdom since under their constitutional monarchy the king has final say over all bills the government debates on. When they opened up to democracy the king only allowed two parties to run, both of which were pro-monarchy.

Memorial Chorten

THE MEMORIAL _CHORTEN_ reflects the centrality of religion to the Bhutanese people's lives. A chorten, also known as a _stupa_, is a sacred ceremonial site, in this case commemorating Bhutan's third king, Jigme Dorji Wangchuck. Built in 1974 this chorten is a focal point for many in Thimphu. It serves a religious role of devotion to the Buddha, but also to the king. It is here that the Buddha and the king are intertwined.

According to Lopen Namgyel, lecturer at Tango Buddhist University, the Bhutanese people see their king as a Buddha in the sense that he has the potential to be a Buddha, but has to be tested first (many people are regarded in such a way in Bhutan). Thanks to its central location in the small city, citizens routinely swing by on their way to or from work or school to do a few *koras* (circumambulation around the chorten), chant their prayers or to do prostrations.

I do a few koras, taking in the peaceful scene around the chorten. Despite being located between a couple of main roads, the place has managed to maintain a certain amount of peacefulness to it, a peacefulness that becomes evident when seeing the many serene elders hanging out there, slowly spinning their prayer wheels as the hours roll by.

Take a Ride and Be Happy

DRIVING WITH LOBSANG reveals still more of the ways spiritual practice is worked into the Bhutanese people's lives. Once in a while there will be a small chorten on the side of the road with a pullout on the other side of it. Lobsang slows the car down and drives along the pullout so as to go around the side of the chorten—not doing a full kora around it (that could get dangerous). The symbolic meaning of this slight detour is all as a reminder. The more times we pull ourselves out of distraction the more we're being in the present moment. Bhutan offers a lot of these reminders, such as the public buses in Thimphu that have "Take a ride and be happy" inscribed on the backs of them.

We drive to Tashi Chho *dzong*. As with other dzongs in Bhutan, Tashi Chho is a dual purpose fortress/monastery that serves both administrative and spiritual functions. And since Bhutan's government is a democracy-monarchy mix this particular dzong in the city's capital acts as both the seat of the civil government as well as the King's throne.

Isolationism and Racism

THIS BUILDING PARALLELS Bhutan's multi-faceted character. As a tiny neighbour sandwiched between India and China it could have easily gotten its culture and traditions steamrolled. Like a tortoise it moves slowly while the two tigers race ahead. To avoid getting eaten up they've taken some pretty substantial measures to protect themselves, like the aforementioned policy on tourism. In addition to that they also banned TV until as recently as 1999. Since democratizing in 2008, Bhutan has relaxed much of its media restrictions, but still does not have any laws in place to guarantee citizens' rights to information.

They have also resorted to some pretty harsh measures to keep their culture intact. The Lhotshampas, the ethnic Nepali minority who started immigrating to Bhutan in the 1800s, were the target of a forced exodus in recent years. Though the Lhotshampas lived in Bhutan for generations, in 1989 the king implemented the One Nation, One People policy aimed against them. According to Human Rights Watch, the Hindu Nepalis were forced to adopt Buddhism, to take on traditional Bhutanese customs, to wear the traditional Bhutanese national clothing and they also stopped teaching Nepali in schools.

They intensified their actions in the '90s by intimidating the Lhotshampas with imprisonment and torture into signing "voluntary migration forms," eventually managing to force an estimated 108,000 of them out to refugee camps in Nepal, where they lived for many years until the UNHCR gave up hope of ever repatriating them back to Bhutan and started exporting them as refugees to other countries, such as the United States, Canada and Australia. It was no easy political situation the current king inherited when he hopped onto the throne in 2008.

Inside the Dzong

AS WE WAIT to be let in to the dzong, the King and Queen come outside to see off some visitors. They wave to the 100 of us foreign tourists, who happily wave back with big smiles. "We love you," shouts one Thai tourist. Regardless of the nationality, it seems royalty has a way of exciting people anywhere in the world.

The dzong is huge. Several mammoth administrative buildings, most of which were closed to the public, enclose multiple courtyards. The main attraction is the monastery. It radiates beauty with grand statues of revered Buddhist figures. The walls are painted with elaborate paintings common to Vajrayana Buddhist monasteries. The prominence of the monastery within the complex points back to the centrality of religion in Bhutan and how it's interweaved with politics.

Assessing Happiness

IMPROVING THE HAPPINESS of a nation is no easy task. First, the question of what happiness is has to be defined. Then there's the issue of appealing to a broad section of society, all with individual needs. Once that's resolved comes the task of developing a framework for improving happiness. To that extent the Bhutanese have done a commendable job for coming up with a set of guidelines that work. And they've implemented much of the ideas they came up with as well. But, there's more to happiness than just that.

Are the Bhutanese really so happy? Most would say they are, particularly when they compare their lives to their neighbours in other south Asian countries. But ask the minority Lhotshampas and they'll give a very different answer.

The Lhotshampa issue opens up a lot of hypocrisy in the Bhutanese claim to be a happy place. Compassion was central to the Buddha's teachings of eradicating suffering—to love others as we love ourselves, which burns a big hole in Bhutan's policy of happiness.

It's a hole worth knowing about. I went to Bhutan knowing about this part of their history. Seeing the country so often marketed as a Shangri-La, I was curious about it. But typical to other ancient societies I've found in south Asia, racism and traditions run very deep, which makes the place a complicated one to understand.

As I sit back into a relaxing drive with Lobsang and Tsering, I absorb the massive vistas of the Himalayan scenery. For every peak there's a valley. That high and low is reflected in all aspects of society, culture and life everywhere in the world. And as any mountain lover can tell you, mountains look far different up close than from far away—they need to be experienced over time and close up to truly appreciate them. It takes time to appreciate Bhutan. And with their complex culture and multifaceted history, it's a good thing they have so many mountains to gaze at in contemplation.

ACCEPTANCE AND EQUANIMITY

A lesson learned from a falling mandarin

AS I WAS WALKING through the Shechen Ogyen Chodzong nunnery in Bhutan with my guides Tsering and Lobsang, a lone mandarin tree dropped one of its few fruit right in front of me. I picked it up and gave it a quick inspection. Part of it was rotten so I tossed it. Tsering remarked that it was good luck for a fruit to drop in front of you so he picked it up, opened it and gave me a piece of its ripe fruit.

The chances of a tree dropping a fruit within a yard of me right as I was walking by are pretty unlikely, particularly since the tree had less than 20 fruit on it. So I understood Tsering's surprise when I ditched it. Though he was guiding me through the South Asian country of Bhutan, on this particular occasion he guided me in another way.

As I savoured that slice of mandarin, I contemplated the value of accepting whatever life offers. There's so much right now that I have in my life. I feel blessed just to have food to eat given all the starvation in the world. I don't need to struggle and strive for so much when I already have so much. I have access to all the basics of life like fresh water, nutritious food and clean air, yet I don't appreciate them nearly enough. And when I don't appreciate what I already have, the value of everything that I end up acquiring diminishes.

We went into the nunnery's main temple where I saw a statue of the Buddha. Tsering pointed out that it had the same face as the Buddha we saw in the previous temple we visited. That same half smile followed me throughout Bhutan from temple to temple, staring me down, prompting me to learn to accept.

67

I interpreted it as a lesson to accept because the Buddha's half smile is one of perfect composure—a state of equanimity that demands a quality of acceptance.

Acceptance is what I feel a true happiness is founded on. And to me true happiness is rooted in equanimity, which is the calm acceptance and joy that is found in any moment, regardless of whether an event is deemed good or bad.

In a state of equanimity, everything that happens is accepted and considered good because the alternatives, struggling after our desires or running away from our aversions is a lifelong trap of discontent.

This connection between acceptance and equanimity was an attitude I found in strong supply throughout Bhutan and elsewhere in South Asia. To be accepting of whatever life gives us demands flexibility, open-mindedness, patience and a good sense of reality. Though acceptance may come as a necessity for those living in hardship in a developing nation, it is a quality well worth developing either way because it helps us master our mind.

Acceptance connects us to equanimity because our perception determines the outcome of every event in our life—one person can see something one way and another the completely opposite way.

In a place like south Asia, the electricity could go off for hours every day and the water supply can easily make you sick. These can be seen as inconveniences or cause for fear, but they can also be seen as the reality to accept and learn from. When life deals out so many difficulties, the mind needs to be managed to generate our own happiness from within.

Being able to endure whatever comes our way is something we can develop through travel (particularly long-term) or living in countries where convenience is not considered a birthright.

Coming from a country where we concern ourselves over luxuries rather than the basics, to take a step back and accept whatever we're given, no matter how dire, transforms what was once previously unacceptable into acceptable. From this perspective our mind learns to stop running from aversions or seeking after desires, but to be happy resting in what is.

TIGER'S NEST

Sublimation and the essence of transformative travel

I WAS MAKING my way steadily up the mountain to Bhutan's most famous site: Tiger's Nest monastery. The prayer flags thickened until I hit a whole wall of them. My vision completely clouded with prayer, my choices were to either go under or find a way around. I did a half limbo until there it was—as if levitating on the side of a cliff, the monastery stood, both a marvel of technical prowess for the careful construction that went into it, and a marvel of human (and animal) effort for the work required to methodically bring the goods up the mountain to this remote location.

Sublime was the only word that came to a mind used to framing experiences in words. This particular word sounded appropriate since it is the root of sublimation. Sublimation is a term used in chemistry to denote a chemical change. The link to alchemy is there. We're constantly changing, but it is by being aware of our changing nature that we find meaning. When we take the time to go on a contemplative trip we place ourselves in one occasion after another that lends itself to reflection, deepening with each experience and reaching further inward.

My guide, Tsering, led me through the monastery, one room after another, each more impressive than the first. I felt a deepening of contemplation coming from the repetition, which was further reinforced by day after day of this same kind of travel, this being the final climactic event of my week in Bhutan.

A number of statues in the monastery held an awe to them, but the one of Guru Rinpoche riding atop his tiger captured my attention. Guru Rinpoche or Padmasambhava is credited with bringing the Vajrayana Buddhist teachings to Bhutan in the 8th century A.D. It is here at Tiger's Nest that he is said to have flown in on his flying tigress.

It wasn't Rinpoche or even the fierce-looking tigress that was overly special but the man underfoot the tigress with his chest ripped open and entrails spilling out that I found myself looking at the most. The meaning of these sometimes frightening statues can be understood in different ways. I've always wondered why the passage of time mythologizes the stories of people like Padmasambhava. But the funny thing is that though these statues make their lives *seem* less real, being at the site where these people lived and did their work and seeing the devotion shown towards them makes them *feel* more real. And right now this statue claimed a powerful effect that my mind hadn't quite comprehended, just felt.

While in one of the temple rooms, Tsering lifted what looked like a trap door in the middle of the floor to reveal a barren rocky part of the cliff where he said Padmasambhava meditated. No luxury accommodation needed for Rinpoche. When he meditated in these barren conditions it seemed he truly forgot about his self.

Sublimation is a process that comes more than anything from effort. Someone could have a near-death experience and have an intense awakening, but without putting effort into understanding the context of that experience, the initial thrill of the experience wears away. The same can be said for any epiphany or realization. Just as a space shuttle launches through the atmosphere the rockets fall back down to Earth and the shuttle soars through space. We want to be the shuttle, not the rockets.

Thinking of masters like Padmasambhava—the man committed himself to an austere life of meditation over who knows how many lifetimes. When he reincarnated as Padmasambhava he was ripe for realization. When I stood at the site where this man lived and worked, the force of this man's effort became apparent to me. He wasn't messing around with his life. He was committed to what he thought was the ultimate way to live, and he did it. His effort was so sublime that he opened up Buddhism to new lands, spurring so many to take the path of sublimation.

Travel can reinforce what we already know, but in a powerfully transformative way. We know the importance of daily practice, whether it's meditation or figure skating, but being in a place where so much effort has been made we can actually feel the legacy left by the master. By feeling the effort they have made (and the many who laboured out of a strong devotion to build such an impressive monastery) it helps drive our own effort forward because it makes real the seemingly distant possibility of enlightenment.

SOBA RIGPA

Good health is all in the mind

A PLAQUE AT the National Institute of Traditional Medicine in Thimphu, Bhutan, summarizes the root cause of illness as being a lack of knowledge of the self.

The traditional form of medicine in this South Asian country is called *Soba Rigpa* (or *gSo-ba Rig-pa*). Dr. Terpola, a doctor working at the Institute's clinic, explains how their medicine works by saying that according to the Tantra, a set of ancient Indian texts, all problems like attachment and ignorance originate in the mind and physical problems then manifest from those problems. It sounds like a broad generalization that could be totally unfounded, but when looking at the power of the mind, using the placebo effect as an example, it becomes easy to see just how much of a role the mind can play in causing illness.

According to Soba Rigpa, the body is composed of three constitutional elements: wind (*lung* – the energy of movement), bile (*thriba* – the energy of digestion) and phlegm (*bethken* – the energy of lubrication and structure). When one of those goes out of whack, a person becomes ill. By harmonizing those three forces in the body wellness returns, but it is the mind that causes these elements to get out of balance in the first place.

In Soba Rigpa, doctors prescribe a number of different herbs and other remedies to treat people. The museum at the Institute of Traditional Medicine houses hundreds of interesting remedies like cordyceps, a funky parasitic fungus that germinates in the larvae of ghost moths and can fetch several thousand dollars per kilogram. This particular fungus is used to treat all kinds of conditions from chronic bronchitis to anemia.

But according to Soba Rigpa, getting over an illness isn't as easy as popping some parasitic fungus. It's about understanding the causes and conditions that cause us to act the way we do and feel the way we do. To Soba Rigpa practitioners the preferred method of understanding the self is Buddhism.

Since Buddhism is the main religion in Bhutan it's the one that people know and trust. But aside from being the traditional option, it's a fine choice for those wanting to understand the self because it offers a deep exploration of the workings of the mind. And the nice thing is, if we learn about how our mind operates not only can we improve our health, we can improve our life in general because we can understand our minds better and not get tricked into believing the stories that we create for ourselves—like being sick.

References:
» The Bhutanese – A Healthy Diet: What Tradition Prescribes
» WebMD – Cordyceps
» NCBI – Traditional Bhutanese medicine (gSo-BA Rig-PA): an integrated part of the formal health care services

sri lanka

SRI PADA PILGRIMAGE

Christmas on Sri Lanka's most sacred mountain

A FEW HUNDRED steps into the Sri Pada pilgrimage route the path steepens. I stick to the far left of the path as I go up, greatly outnumbered by the flood of people coming down. An elderly woman in an all-white sari hobbles down the crumbling stone steps locked arm in arm with her teenage grandson. A woman in her third trimester descends just as slowly, her patient husband dutifully clutching her by the arm as he negotiates every irregular step for them.

Countless parents lug their passed out toddlers over their shoulders or carry them in their arms, the dead weight making for an exhausting journey. Pilgrims lay stretched out in makeshift rest houses along the way. The wooden benches will not keep them there for long, just enough to replenish their energy before they make their way back down. Some tend to their aching muscles with the local Ayurvedic equivalent of Tiger Balm while others line the side of the path head down resting on their knees for a much-needed micro-break.

These pilgrims are among the thousands every day who climb the mountain called Sri Pada or Adam's Peak, depending on who you ask. For more than 1000 years Buddhists, Muslims, Christians and Hindus have made the trip to the top of this mountain in central Sri Lanka.

The island's majority Buddhist population reveres Sri Pada for the footprint the Buddha left on the peak as he went off to paradise. But the island's Muslims contest the Buddhists' claim, calling it Adam's Peak to commemorate the spot where Adam landed when he was cast out of paradise. Christians believe the footprint belonged to St. Thomas and finally, Hindus say it was actually Shiva's footprint.

Whoever's footprint it was, Sri Lanka's diverse religious groups all climb the mountain day and night, respecting each others individual spiritual traditions. With four of the world's major religions peacefully climbing the mountain, Sri Pada is considered a sanctuary for all faiths. In fact, according to Ven. S. Dhammika, no mountain, not even Mount Sinai or Kailash, has been revered by so many people from so many different spiritual traditions, for as long as Sri Pada.

I had opted for a 3 a.m. start to catch sunrise after hearing about the spectacular view from up top. The path is lit by overhead lamps that stretch up into the night sky—light, light, light, star. We truly are walking a path to the stars on this clear, pleasantly cool night. "Merry Christmas," a young Sri Lankan man greets me as he descends, guessing that my white skin must mean I'm Christian. He's right. Though I'm not a practicing Christian, the decision to spend this Christmas, my first away from home, wasn't an easy one. I give him a big smile and respond to the greeting.

I stop at one of the many roti shops along the way and talk to one of the few non-Sri Lankan pilgrims, a young Japanese woman named Nao (pronounced "now"). I remark on the auspiciousness of her name. I am grateful for this reminder to be in the now to fully appreciate this memorable occasion.

Approaching the top of the mountain, the numbers turn. Most had been going down, but now the majority of people are heading up. I reach the top where hundreds are standing on the steps filling every square foot of the peak while others perch on the ledge of the lower temple, all facing eastwards in anticipation of the sun's arrival.

The first glow of the rising sun pierces the darkness of the night as I take up my position among the pilgrims. We stand in near silence as the sun rises. Deep hues of red and pink cut holes through a pocket of low-hanging cloud as a nearby lake reflects the image of the clear, blue sky in its perfect stillness.

Church bells from the nearest village fill my ears on this Christmas morning. As hundreds of pilgrims shuffle past me to pay their respects and give their offerings to Sri Pada at the top, I sit on the peak staring out at the panorama of lush mountainous jungle as I feel the sun's rays quickly warming up the crisp morning air.

I eventually make it to the temple to offer my donation to the Buddha. I queue beside a young guy from Colombo who came on a road trip with his friends. I remark how amazing it is that a group of guys in their twenties use their holiday time to take a trip where the source of entertainment is spending time with the Buddha.

We arrive at the front of the line. Two attendants quickly usher us through as I drop my donation and bow to the Buddha. The whole donate-bow rush seems kind of weird, especially when it's presided over by a monk sitting in the temple's alcove raking the cash and coins like a Vegas dealer, but it's really the only conceivable way this popular pilgrimage can go down.

Sri Pada is an island-wide pilgrimage. Over the five-month pilgrimage season, a good chunk of the island's population make it up at least once. To Sri Lankans it's more a rite than a choice. Most take a long bus ride from their homes, do the long hike—often all at night—then head immediately home. While it may be uncomfortable to climb the mountain in the rain or inconvenient to take time off their busy work schedules, they just do it.

As I make my descent I meet Gayan, another guy road tripping from Colombo with his crew. We talk Buddhism the whole way down. He puts the pilgrimage in perspective. The Sri Lankan Buddhist tradition is to offer flowers to the Buddha. By offering flowers, which are a symbol of perfection, he offers his greatest virtues to the Buddha and in so doing connects to those virtues in himself.

He does the pilgrimage every year at this time as a way of extending that offering over a period of several hours rather than several minutes at regular temple visits. His view, however, is just one of many—the view varies as much among people of the same spiritual tradition as between them.

Pilgrimages are representative of the spiritual path in general. Why bother doing it? It's like asking "Who am I?" It's not a question that needs to be asked in order to live, but in doing so people can come to their own version of the truth.

Truth for me as a practicing Buddhist comes through a Buddhist lens. But as a born Christian, Christmas holds special significance. This day brought the two together in a special way. As I spent the day in quiet contemplation, I saw the different faiths gathered together showing their devotion. One religion or another it doesn't matter. Contemplation and devotion are the same no matter the spiritual tradition.

KANDYAN DANCE

Sri Lanka's captivating traditional dance form

CONSIDERED SRI LANKA'S greatest cultural export, Kandyan dance was almost lost during the period of British rule due to the cultural domination imposed by the ruling empire. Good thing it's been revived because it is one truly captivating show that would be a shame if it were lost.

Dancers adorned with rattling anklets, elaborate beads, jingling bangles, funky headgear and colourful flowing costumes perform stunning high jumps and summersaults while drummers flank them, pounding out heart-thumping tribal rhythms. With a stage set amid the deep, lush jungle of Sri Lanka, a Kandyan dance performance captures the imagination by connecting audiences to their tribal roots.

Kandyan dance is said to have spawned from an exorcism ritual that Indian shamans brought to the island at the request of the king who was suffering from a mysterious illness many years ago.

As the legend goes, the king was experiencing a recurring dream that was causing him much anguish, which he believed to be black magic working against him. After the dance was performed for him, his mystery illness disappeared—and from then forward, the dance flourished.

Kandyan dance has different forms, such as *ves*, a sacred dance in devotion to the god Kohomba; *uddeki*, which gets its name from the small hourglass-shaped hand drum that's played for the dance; and *vannams*, which has vocal recitations to express the virtues of the animals being depicted.

With the exception of vannams, traditional Kandyan dance is paired solely to the sounds of the drum and other percussion instruments such as cymbals. The *tammettama* is one such instrument, a twin drum played with thin cane drumsticks as well as the two-sided *geta beraya* drum. The combination of the two drums and cymbals are enough to fill the space with full, richly textured sound.

Though Kandyan dance has traditionally been reserved for men, today women commonly perform it and have adapted their own style of costume. The success of Kandyan dance has resulted in its both spreading beyond the city of Kandy for which it's named (still the best place to watch it) and has spawned various dance schools as well as being integrated into other forms of contemporary dance in Sri Lanka and beyond. As the national dance of Sri Lanka, it lives on as an enduring feature of a country richly endowed with culture.

SLOW TRAVEL IN SRI LANKA

Slow down your pace to experience the culture of the place

SLOW TRAVEL DOESN'T always mean taking months or years off work to ramble around the world. It's a frame of mind. A matter of choice. Do we choose the drive-thru or parking our car and ordering inside. Better yet, how about staying in and cooking at home.

Cooking at home was just what I did at Rani's Inn in Negombo, Sri Lanka—a kitchen opportunity I never would have had if I'd just torn through town as most people do in Negombo.

With its proximity to the airport, the beachside town has unfortunately become known as the place to crash when you get off the plane. A spot to spend a night or two upon first arriving in Sri Lanka, which doesn't suffer from the oppressive traffic and pollution of Colombo.

There are better beaches in Sri Lanka, better places for sightseeing and probably better restaurants too. So, yes, the guidebooks are justified in marking it as a stopover point.

Where the guidebooks fall short, however, (as they typically do) is in capturing the human aspect of the place, the culture, the people. It's the people that make a place and by extension, it's the people that generally make a trip special. Beautiful beaches can be found anywhere in the world. Same with mountains, lakes, cities and shopping malls. Sites of historical and cultural significance are great to see, but if it's culture you're after, it's not all bound up in a 2000-year-old tomb or the made-for-tourists dance performances.

Checking out those attractions is great, not knocking them, but they only illuminate one side of a nation's culture, and in the case of Sri Lanka, the ancient, not the living, breathing, present.

I stuck around Negombo for two weeks. Though not long, it was a lot longer than most travellers spend. During my stay I saw many people come and go. It's a sight the locals get used to, which gives them an excuse to not know your name, and for some, a reason to rip you off.

In my time there I befriended Gayan, a local waiter about my age, hung out at the local joints and met some of his friends. I danced on the beach with the locals. I learned how to make the Sri Lankan staple, rice and curry, and I heard the story of Maurice, a fisherman who lost everything in the 2004 tsunami and was voraciously practicing his English every chance he got. His goal: to get out of poverty and get his two teenage kids the education he didn't get.

Slowly moving through a place need not take much time, just more time than usual. Enough time for the people to open up and call you a friend. One of the most beautiful aspects of travel is the element of surprise. Slow down your pace where most people wouldn't to uncover treasures that otherwise would have gone unseen.

nepal

PILGRIMAGE OF PEACE

Lumbini, Nepal—the site of the Buddha's birth

ASK MOST PEOPLE where the Buddha was from and they'll tell you India. Ask a Nepali and they'll be quick to point out that Siddhartha Gautama, better known as the Buddha, was indeed born in present-day Nepal, though he did spend most of his life living in India.

Nepal has done a fine job preserving the tranquil pilgrimage site of Lumbini, known to Buddhists around the world as the birthplace of the Buddha. Situated amid a buffer zone of 22 square miles of parkland, the Lumbini Development Zone is home to the Maya Devi Temple (the site where the Buddha was born), an Ashoka Pillar (a monument erected by King Ashoka to commemorate his visit to the pilgrimage area) as well as Buddhist *viharas* and *stupas* that date back to the third century BC and a sacred bathing pool called Puskarni where the Buddha's mother Maya Devi took a bath before she gave birth.

The pilgrimage site emanates a peaceful vibe that comes from centuries of pilgrims spending time there in devotion and quiet contemplation. But step back from the main site and there's much to appreciate. One temple after another the pilgrim or curious traveller can roam through Lumbini's development zone, slowly taking in the sites and paying respect to the Buddha in temples from just about every country in the world that has a significant Buddhist presence. Aside from checking out Buddhist art and architecture from around the world, another nice thing about the temples is that they're situated among the jungle, which makes for a nice quiet bike ride or walk.

If spending more than a day or two at Lumbini it's worth making the side trip to Kapilvastu, also known as Tilaurakot. Twenty-seven kilometres from Lumbini this is the site of the Buddha's palace growing up, and the spot where he left his wife and child to renounce everything in his life in search of the ultimate truth. Though there's not much to actually see in Kapilvastu aside from ruins, it holds a special importance to Buddhists and makes for a nice place to spend quiet time and reflect, as it gets few tourists—quite different than the main site.

As Buddhism is one of the fastest growing religions in the world, its pilgrimage sites are feeling the burden. Lumbini is no different. The village may soon experience a major building boom if the planned "World Peace City" goes through, transforming the once quiet village with lots of parkland to a city of a quarter million.

Development or not, Lumbini holds such importance as a sacred pilgrimage site for Buddhists that makes it well worth visiting, and for those interested in meditation, a selection of meditation courses available at different monasteries and meditation centres, coupled with the peaceful surroundings make it a great spot to do a Vipassana course or other meditation program.

TRANSCENDENT BEAUTY

From Pokhara to Sarangkot, Nepal

THERE ARE SOME places where natural beauty is so potent that experiencing it can bring a person to a higher place. Pokhara is one of those places. The front side faces Phewa Lake and the opposite side backs onto the massive Annapurna range. Despite being 28 km away, these mountains are so high that if you stand on the opposite side of the lake you can actually see their reflection in the water—a photographer's dream, a mountain gazer's fantasy, a poet's inspiration.

Some travellers visit Pokhara and never leave. With some of the best paragliding in Asia, paddling on the lake, trekking in the nearby Annapurna National Park, volunteering at local NGOs, there's something to do for just about everyone. And plenty of options for those who want to do just about nothing: relaxing by the lakeside, meditating in the Buddhist meditation centre, strolling through the park, sampling wonderful international cuisine. There's a good number of long-term travellers and expats who have settled in Pokhara, particularly the north end of the lake, for these many reasons.

It's easy to get caught up in the beauty of Pokhara, and to get comfortable there, which is not a bad option in the least. But for those wanting a deeper natural and cultural immersion they can either go trekking in the mountains, doing a different homestay every night, or settle into a village.

Sitting atop the nearest mountain just outside of Pokhara, Sarangkot is a village that is both close and far away. Convenient and rustic. It's a nice hour or two hike from Pokhara Lakeside or a short drive, but it feels like it's a world away with the quietude of nature and the peaceful vibe of the village. It used to be the first stop on the classic Annapurna circuit, but since a road was built a few years back linking Pokhara to a point closer to the park, the tourist numbers have dropped. The village retains its charm as there are a few guest houses but not too many, and the ones that are there blend into the landscape pretty well.

The panoramic view of the Annapurna range from Sarangkot is one of the most easily accessible views of massive mountains (8,000m+) in the world. Sarangkot is billed in the guidebooks as a place to visit for a night and see the sunrise. Though the sunrise is spectacular (if you're lucky enough to have a clear morning) it's easy to stay more than a night.

Hospitable, amiable and cheerful, the people of Sarangkot make travellers feel at home. Stick around a bit and take part in their daily life: try carrying bales of hay on your back Nepali-style, carry some rocks for home building or do some gardening. The road linking it to adjacent villages doesn't see many vehicles and is relatively flat, making it a fine road to go for a run or easy walk. Add to that the view, which is on the Pokhara valley side, makes for a nice change from the mountain view.

With its gift of elevation, Sarangkot cranks the beauty up a notch. Viewed from above, the lake is an even more spectacular sight, the view of the mountains is perhaps the best view of that range from any other point since it provides an unobstructed panorama, and you have a full view of Pokhara Valley and surrounding mountains. The beauty of this place is like a tranquilizer that can transform stress to peace. And if you stick around awhile it's easy to absorb the cheerful contentedness that the villagers readily display in their warm smiles.

VILLAGE THERAPY

Learning to live at the pace of "just enough" in Thakurdwara

I WOKE TO THE SOUND of a bomb blast. Not an explode your eardrum kind of vibration. More like a really loud firecracker. Though it happened nearby I didn't hear anyone yelling and screaming. No loud noises. Nothing. So I didn't make much of it. But despite the peacefulness of the surroundings I couldn't help feeling a little unsettled.

I was in the village of Thakurdwara, adjacent to Bardia National Park in remote western Nepal. This country had been through hell in recent years with civil warfare forcing its citizens into hiding on a regular basis. Particularly hard hit were remote rural areas like this one. Bomb blasts were a way of life. Something they got so used to that they'd barely flinch at the sound of one.

Election day observances

IT WAS ELECTION DAY and the Maoist dissidents were trying to scare voters into not going out and voting on this critical ballot, a much-anticipated national election that would finally unite the leaderless nation behind a prime minister—a post that had effectively been vacant for nearly two years. It was also a vote that would allow for the creation of a new constitution that the country had longed for since the end of the civil war.

It was already light outside when the bomb went off so I decided to get up and see what was going on. I asked some locals about it…. turns out it was just a pressure cooker bomb. A homemade job where they'd grab their mother's pressure cooker from the kitchen,

91

stuff some nails and explosive materials into it and set it off with a simple cooking timer.

With everyone on high alert due to the election, someone spotted the cooker and reported it to the police, who conducted a controlled explosion. No one was hurt.

I later heard about a second bomb that went off just outside the village. I slept through it so it couldn't have been that loud. No one got hurt with that one either.

So all in all, a regular day at the polls in Nepal. Local villagers went about their business and did their voting as part of their daily routine. All was normal in this otherwise peaceful village. This stunned me. A bomb went off and everything was just so… normal. Peaceful, calm, smiles all around. The villagers' sense of contentment, despite the daily hardship they endure, was what truly intrigued me about this place. I wanted to know how these people live and how they developed such a strong sense of equanimity.

Tiger trekking

WHAT BROUGHT ME to Bardia was the possibility of spotting a tiger in the wild. And not just any tiger sighting, Bardia is one of the few places in the world where you can do tiger treks. Just you, your guide, two bamboo sticks and nothing else to walk through the jungle.

And it's not just tigers milling around. This park is home to elephants, leopards, crocodiles, rhinos. Though I wasn't one of the lucky ones who got to see a tiger I did see a wild elephant walking close to us, flocks of hornbills flying overhead, herds of spotted deer, langurs (what the locals call the black-faced monkey) and a colourful variety of birds.

I spent a good amount of time hiking around the park whether looking for tigers or leopards. Even though the chances of encountering a big cat are slim, there's something thrilling about walking through tiger country on foot.

The bombing brought its sizzle of excitement to the village as well. But while there was no shortage of excitement on this trip to

Thakurdwara, what I truly remember about the place was quite the opposite.

Village people, peaceful people

WHAT STRUCK ME was the peacefulness of the village. Every day I would walk around the village of Thakurdwara and see the same faces. Them regularly saying "hello" (usually the only English word they knew so they got quite good at saying it) as I walked by. Sometimes the conversation extended to "Where are you from?" or the other typical question, "Are you married?" Usually followed with a "Why not?" Being a solo traveler, particularly one in his mid-thirties, I'm easy prey for people's curiosity/pity.

I saw a lot of smiles. Kids riding their bikes aimlessly around the village. Young women carrying massive pots on their heads. Old ladies sitting outside the house, talking and observing the goings on around them. Guys doing construction work on the house. They were just going about their daily routines, day in day out, but doing it with such a contentedness that I couldn't help feel some envy towards them.

I didn't see cars driving around the outer part of the village where I normally walked. There were just dirt paths through the jungle and along the stream. This meant no cars and just the odd motorbike that would whiz past. For the most part people walked and rode bicycles.

This brought the pace of life down to a sensible level. It was slow, but things moved fast enough to get things done. The routes were not clear-cut straightaways that spell efficiency and nothing else. No, the paths had just enough circuity to them to slow you down and get you to appreciate your surroundings. To meander through neighbours' fields and see them as you walk by. To not get stuck on auto-pilot.

The village was just the right size. It was all walkable and the heart of the village was just a couple of small roads. Large enough to get the daily shopping done but small enough to see the same faces and get to know people.

Living with just enough

THERE'S A CONTENTEDNESS in the air that even regular bomb blasts or being forced into hiding cannot quell. It seems nothing can erase the smiles on these people's faces because they've found contentment living a life of "just enough."

These people don't have much. Families live in tiny one-room dwellings. They eat *dal bhat* (rice and beans) day in, day out. They have poor access to health care, they have minimal road access, they haul heavy loads around all day and they work hard under high heat.

I'm in no way romanticizing poverty, but I've found a great amount of positive in their way of life to learn from.

There's a powerful effect that comes from being immersed in nature and being in tune with its natural rhythms. Get up at dawn, go in at dusk. Walking instead of driving. Moving at the pace of cows and goats... having cows and goats. Eat fresh food and breathe clean air. Live among a minimal amount of people in tribal harmony, unencumbered by useless shit and useless thoughts. No need to race here to do this or that or whatever other pointless crap we find to occupy ourselves.

These things seem like a small deal, but they actually have a massive impact. Every time I observe life in a village, and to a lesser extent in a town, I encounter the same phenomenon. It's the same thing elsewhere in Nepal, elsewhere in South Asia and elsewhere in all developing nations I've been to.

Memories from Bardia

IF I HAD ACTUALLY seen a tiger that probably would have been the most memorable moment of my time in Bardia. But instead, what I remember most was meeting a 10-year-old girl on one of my walks through the village who knew somewhat more than "hello" English. And she was eager to practice what she knew. I'd seen her a couple of times. The first time she followed the standard, "Are you married," "Why not?" routine. But on the last time, when I told her I was leaving, she spoke to me as if she were a wise old lady sitting in her rocking chair doling out advice.

"Find a girl and come back," she said. To add emphasis and urgency to her words she stared in my eyes and repeated them with the confidence of someone who surely knows what's best for me.

The reason why this struck me so deeply is because here's this 10-year-old girl who spoke with such firmness of purpose that she could have been her age in dog years. For her, meeting a man, getting married, starting a family and living the life she knew to live was her dharma, her duty in life. She knew what she had to do to live out her time on this Earth and be content. There's just no question about it to her. She spoke with a resoluteness of purpose that I wish I had.

There are indeed issues with having a lack of choice so I'm not going to whine like a privileged Westerner about how having so much choice is a curse. I've been granted choice and that choice has enabled me in ways that previously were unthinkable even a generation ago. I'm massively grateful for that. But there's a point where questioning, searching, exploring, dreaming, wondering "What my purpose in life is" goes just too far and starts to work against you.

Wandering around this part of the world has helped me find and know with that same firm resoluteness what my duty in this life is. It's a story for another day. Today, I close this chapter by showing gratitude for Nepal, India, Sri Lanka and Bhutan. They have all been my gurus.

I have gained a great respect for people who can live contentedly in a state of equanimity, making the most of the little they have. I see the importance of their connection to nature and respect of traditions. I realize the value of going slow and doing what matters in life and cutting out the rest. I have learned the importance of being happy with your life as is.

The struggle for happiness is one we put a lot of energy trying to figure out and strive towards. For that reason, of all the lessons I learned on this subcontinent, this lesson of just enough is the greatest lesson of them all.

Visit The Mindful Word to read more
of Kiva Bottero's transformative
travel stories.

www.themindfulword.org

Printed in Great Britain
by Amazon